THE ABSTRACT SOCIETY

ANTON C. ZIJDERVELD was born in Malang, Indonesia, attended the gymnasium in Utrecht, Holland, and received his Ph.D. degree in sociology from the University of Leiden. He has also studied at the Hartford Seminary Foundation in Connecticut. From 1966 to 1968 he was assistant professor of sociology and anthropology at Wagner College, New York, and he is now associate professor of sociology at Sir George Williams University in Montreal.

THE ABSTRACT SOCIETY

*A Cultural Analysis
of Our Time*

by
ANTON C. ZIJDERVELD

JAY
ANCHOR BOOKS

DOUBLEDAY & COMPANY, INC.
GARDEN CITY, NEW YORK

The Abstract Society was originally published in hardcover by Doubleday & Company, Inc., in 1970.

Anchor Books edition: 1971

4/12/00   SBEN   CAM6179

To Peter L. Berger and Hans C. Hoekendijk

Die ungeheure Grausamkeit unserer politischen und wirtschaftlichen Organisationsform, die den Gefuehlen des Einzelnen Gewalt antut, ist so unentrinnbar, weil diese Organisation zur gleichen Zeit dem Einzelnen ueberhaupt erst eine Oberflaeche und die Moeglichkeit eines Ausdrucks gibt. Denn man kann sagen, der Mensch wird erst durch den Ausdruck, und dieser formt sich in den Formen der Gesellschaft.

Robert Musil
Der Deutsche Mensch als
Symptom (Hamburg: Rowohlt
Verlag, 1967), p. 21

The enormous cruelty of our political and economic social structures, which do violence to the feelings of individuals, is so unescapable because these very social structures at the same time give the individual a shape and the possibility of an expression. Thus, one might say that man becomes man only through expression that is formed in the context of social structures.

(Translation by Professor Kurt Jonassohn)

ACKNOWLEDGMENTS

This book is dedicated to two of my teachers. I would contradict its main conclusion, if this dedication were amplified by emotional expressions of gratitude. Silence, on the other hand, would border on treason. I therefore take this opportunity to mention the existential and intellectual impact of Peter L. Berger and Hans C. Hoekendijk on my biography and on my writing.

The heights and depths of our friendships, marked by the problems of mind and life that each of us seem to share, are of a private nature and may be passed by here. More has to be said about their influence on my intellectual development. Nobody can claim any patents in matters of ideas, but those who profit by them should at least mention the sources.

Hans Hoekendijk helped me in my transition from theology to sociology during our common years at the University of Utrecht. He has always stimulated me without any reservations since he knew that my decision to forsake theology was dictated by intellectual necessity. His passionate involvement in the problems of contemporary society has left behind a lasting impression. Peter Berger introduced me to the discipline of sociology in his phenomenal way. I had been initiated in the basic principles of empirical sociology before I met him, but it was only after I worked with him as a teaching assistant that the demon of sociological inquisitiveness took hold of me.

The reader who knows Peter Berger's *Invitation to Sociology* (1963) and his systematic sociology of knowledge, written in collaboration with Thomas Luckmann (*The Social Construction of Reality,* 1966) can judge for himself how much Berger's thinking and approach influenced mine. Here I want to stress only that it was Berger who, in 1963–64, opened my eyes to the dialectic nature of the relationship between man and society. This was the basis for my Dutch dissertation in which I investigated the methodological

implications of the dialectic nature of the process of institutionalization (*Institutionalisering*, 1966) and it is again the
fundamental frame of reference for the present discussion.
In a sociology of knowledge, as outlined by Berger and Luckmann, the *homo duplex* theorem is bound to become an
essential theoretical problem (which was recently shown by
Luckmann in his *The Invisible Religion*, 1967). In this book
I shall make an attempt to use this theorem for an interpretive understanding of man's position in and reaction to
modern society. One can see this argument as an application
of the notions of sociology of knowledge to the field of social
philosophy.

I am much in debt to Professor Ely Chinoy for his reading
of earlier drafts of the manuscript. Several comments of his
have helped to clarify my arguments. Numerous discussions
with my colleague and friend Professor Joseph Smucker had
a profound impact on the writing of this book. Intellectual
influences like these do usually not occur in footnotes, thus
they deserve a special mention. I am grateful to Miss Gisela
Preusser and Miss Rachela Handsman for their assistance in
the typing of the manuscript.

It has become customary for an author in academia to
thank his wife for her invaluable contributions to his intellectual creations—mostly under the silent assumption that these
creations are important enough to make such a statement
mandatory. Not without satisfaction, my wife and I came to
the conclusion that a statement like "without her this book
could not have been written" would be presumptuous and
even false. This book was written in periods of solitary con-
finement in the author's office out of which he was often liberated by his wife. These interruptions may have delayed the
appearance of the book, but they prevented me from the
serious threat of becoming a sociological monomaniac.

PREFACE

Despite obvious and profound differences, the three "founding fathers" of modern sociology, Karl Marx, Émile Durkheim, and Max Weber, shared one basic concern. Each in his own way tried to determine the nature of the relationship between man and modern society. Marx focused on the freedom of man and the threat of alienation. Durkheim, from a totally different perspective, centered his analyses around such problems as the need for institutional order and the dangers of anomie. Obviously, neither of them separated analytic sociology from normative social philosophy carefully enough, and in this respect they lacked the methodological aloofness of Max Weber.

Weber's emphasis on the value-freedom and objectivity of the social sciences meant a strict separation of two essentially different frames of reference: the empirical realm of analytic sociology on the one hand and the normative realm of social philosophy, social ethics and politics on the other. In his sociology one finds hardly any theories about the threat of alienation or the dangers of anomie since statements about such problems can be made only on the basis of subjective values and normative convictions. Weber, of course, never said that values and convictions are irrelevant. They simply do not belong to the scientific frame of reference.

This is not to say, however, that Weber in a positivistic mood disengaged himself from the socio-philosophical and socio-ethical problems of man in modern society. On the contrary, all of his historical and analytic sociology can be seen as a continuous attempt to understand the nature of Western society, its increasing rationalization and the unique position of man in this society.

This has set the stage for modern empirical sociology. A merging of sociology and social philosophy, or of analysis and praxis (as respectively in Durkheim and Marx) is hardly possible after Weber. If it occurs, as it does among many New Left philosophers, confusion instead of meaningful understanding is the price to be paid. Weber's methodological aloofness, however, may easily lead to "one-dimensional" positivism, particularly among less gifted sociologists. In that case, value-freedom degenerates into naïveté, confining the social sciences to irrelevance on the problems of man in modern society. Indeed, much of contemporary sociology is remote from Weber's agonizing search for an understanding of modern man and Western civilization.

It is my firm conviction that sociology as an empirical discipline can maintain its value as an objective science only if it remains relevant with regard to the problems of man and modern society. That means that, after having accepted Weber's principle of value-freedom, the sociologist should dare to transcend the methodological limits of his discipline and confront such problems as alienation, anomie and dehumanization. Social philosophy and social ethics are the proper fields for such a confrontation.

Weber can be productive today only if the spirit of Marx and Durkheim with their humanistic zeal is added to his analytic rationalism. This is possible because essentially, although not ostentatiously, Weber was driven by the same zeal. This then is the task I have set myself in the present book.

CONTENTS

THE ABSTRACT SOCIETY

THE NEED
FOR CULTURAL ANALYSIS

Max Scheler characterized man as a being able to say no.[1]
Unlike the animal who is trapped in his world, man tries
continuously to transcend the limits of his body, his mind,
his physical environment, and his tradition by refusing to
accept them as facts and taken-for-granted realities. Similarly, though in a different frame of reference, Albert Camus
asserted that man is the only creature in nature who refuses
to be what he is. Parodying Descartes' famous theorem in
an existentialist way, he exclaimed: "Je me révolte, donc
nous sommes."[2] Rebellion and revolt are thus seen as an
essential human feature. One could, for instance, also mention the numerous philosophies of revolution from Marx to
Sartre, or the ideological impact of practical revolutionaries
like Che Guevara on the intelligentsia of the New Left.

This picture of man as a revolutionary or rebel differs
quite remarkably from most sociological observations on
modern man's alleged conformism. We live, we are told, in
a technological and industrial society which tries to mold
us to uniform patterns. The functionary, the organization
man, the bureaucratic apparatchik, and the worker at the
assembly line all have to obey the rules and norms of their
systems. They produce and accomplish competitively in a
strict and hierarchic order. Because of this competition and
hierarchy, they can hardly afford to rebel. Therefore, conformism and adjustment seem to characterize the nature of
modern man far better than protest and revolt. If this were
true, the sociologist could dismiss the philosophical theory
of man as a metaphysical delusion. He could point at the
human need for adaptation to social institutions and restrict
his analyses to the functions of the institutional structures,

their integration and their social control. Indeed, in much of contemporary sociology man appears as a player of pre-defined roles who obeys the demands of social systems.

However, if the sociologist cares to look at the protest movements of the sixties which roll through industrial societies in ever-stronger waves, and if he is willing to take these protests into serious consideration, he must concede that modern man's conformism and adjustments are clearly limited. Apparently man is not infinitely malleable and may eventually decide to say "no" to his socio-cultural environment. The sociologist facing this fact is forced to raise some very fundamental philosophical and socio-ethical questions about man's place in society, his relation to the "objective" world of institutions, and the meaning and freedom he is searching for in a socio-cultural reality which he created and has to maintain with his fellow men.

It is important to realize that actually both points of view hold true for contemporary industrial society. An analysis of man's situation in modern society cannot overlook two contrary attitudes: there is conformism and there is protest, there are adjustments to existing circumstances and there are revolts against these circumstances. It is hardly necessary to repeat that modern man is constantly molded and manipulated psychologically, socially, culturally, politically and economically by highly complex, abstract structures. But ever stronger protests against this demanding society and its allegedly alienating forces can be observed. One really does not have to be a hippie or student activist to understand the spirit of protest that moves so many of the younger generation today.

This paradox of societal manipulation and human protest characterized the sixties and will probably dominate the next decade of Western civilization. This book proposes to interpret the paradox within one frame of reference, the so-called *homo duplex* theorem. Since this theoretical framework lies beyond the limits and boundaries of empirical sociology, I must first explain the methodological assumptions that guided my argument. In doing so, I take the opportunity to elaborate on the remark about social philosophy and social ethics I made at the end of the preface.

Social scientists usually show a remarkable ability to ignore philosophical questions as to the actual state of affairs of the society and culture in which they are living. Before we scorn them for that, we should keep in mind that they have to refrain from philosophical problems in order to remain scientific. The fundamental rule of scientific analysis is objectivity and value-freedom. The influence of subjective values cannot be denied (particularly in the case of the social sciences), but its absence is sought for as the ideal situation. In order to be genuinely scientific, the social scientist has to stick to the facts as strictly as possible and therefore suspend philosophical interpretations.

But he also has to live with these facts. Social phenomena cannot be viewed as merely objects for disinterested research. They are constitutive parts of our very existence: we make them, they make us. Their substance, their "flesh and blood" consist of you and me and the others. In short, we make society, society makes us. Thus the question must be raised whether we make society and society makes us in a *human* way. When the social scientist asks this question, he transcends the limits set by the methodological demands of his discipline. He moves from the analytical to the interpretive frame of reference; from the realm of value-free objectivity to an intellectual climate in which normative value judgments can no longer be evaded.

At this point, it might be helpful to recall Georg Simmel's argument about the relationship between sociology and philosophy. Sociology as an empirical discipline, according to Simmel, is flanked by philosophy. On one side lies methodology (the epistemology and logic of sociology) and on the other social philosophy (or social metaphysics). As methodology, philosophy asks for the presuppositions and methods of sociological analysis; as social philosophy, it tries to place the sociological elements in a holistic and general framework in order to reach an understanding of the nature of man and society.[3]

The step from the analytical to the normative is permissible, it seems to me, as long as it is made consciously and on methodological grounds. One could argue that it is even methodologically mandatory, since it contributes to an improvement of the scientific understanding of man and society. If the social scientist remains blind to the fact that social phenomena bear on his and others' existential position in society, he may very well end up with a primitive philosophy that makes him believe that the empirically gathered facts (the bewildering amount of data he drew from reality) and the theoretically constructed models (the shaky hypotheses of an artificial nature) constitute life and social reality. This sociological positivism, the belief that gathered data and constructed models can be taken as a full account of life and society, is the basic philosophy of too many social scientists and represents a fatal form of social metaphysics. It is one of the most fallacious distortions of genuinely objective and empirical research. Afraid of metaphysics, these empiricists retreat to a positivistic standpoint where they are not aware of the value judgments and normative assumptions that "secretly" enter their research and theoretical models.

To those who are convinced of the necessity for value-free analysis, this transition from the methodological limits of the sociological discipline to an interpretive and critical understanding of man's position in modern society might seem rather dangerous. Having the examples of social philosophers like Spengler or Toynbee and their romantic accounts of cultural decay and deterioration of Western civilization, one could legitimately hesitate to leave the relatively safe realm of one's discipline. Surely, if one transcends the barriers of science, the result might well be science fiction or clairvoyance. It is infinitely safer for the intellectually honest sociologist to stick to the data and ignore all questions that transcend the objective analysis of facts. But in that case he might end up with a primitive positivism and naïve optimism about the actual problems of man and modern society, leaving the sound scrutiny of these problems to journalists, prophets, and clairvoyants. It seems to me to be a matter of responsibility and intellectual courage to dare to make the step from social science to social philosophy and social ethics. Prophets and clairvoyants generally do not care to listen carefully to the facts. They use data selectively in order to "prove" their theoretical constructions. Social scientists, on the other hand, are still too much enchanted by the empiricist cult of data. Both pitfalls are to be avoided in a discussion of those problems with which the present book is going to deal.

In this book I shall attempt to read and interpret some of the most conspicuous signs of our time, namely the increasing autonomy of abstract social structures vis-à-vis a spreading spirit of protest against these structures on the part of the modern individual. One can call this enterprise a study in *cultural analysis* which is based on sociological observations but philosophical in nature. As such, it continues the thoughts and observations of two European cultural analysts who always remained in touch with empirical facts but transcended them in order to grasp more encompassing and general problems. I am referring to Karl Mannheim's *Man and Society in an Age of Reconstruction,* written in the turmoil of the thirties,[4] and to the less famous cultural analysis of the German-Danish sociologist Theodor Geiger, called *Demokratie ohne Dogma (Democracy without Doctrine,* originally published under the title *Society between Pathos and Soberness),*[5] written shortly after the Second World War and published for the first time in 1950. These two studies illustrate the kind of analysis I had in mind in writing this book, which should be seen in the tradition of Mannheim and Geiger.

Mannheim, who showed deep concern for the political and cultural situation of Western civilization in books like *Diagnosis of Our Time* (1943) and *Ideology and Utopia* (1936), tries in *Man and Society in an Age of Reconstruction* (1940) to analyze sociologically the main changes in the social structure of modern society. But he leaves the field of analytic theory and reaches a more comprehensive interpretation when he turns to the problems man encounters in these changes and to the faults of the social structures. Reduced to its essence, the main problem of modern society appears to be a dilemma that stems from the fact that the principle of *laissez-faire* (i.e. the liberal search for individual freedom) has become obsolete, leaving room for all kinds of totalitarianism. Thus more than ever before, the individual is threatened by the dictatorship of single individuals or of classes and groups. Bewildered by the political and social turmoil of the late thirties in Europe, the disenchanted liberal Mannheim drew the conclusion that "a radical change of structure" was taking place which required a drastic reconstruction of the individual and of society.

We are in a better position today to evaluate Mannheim's observations, which were inspired by an admirable humanistic zeal. Instead of the reconstruction he was pleading for, the destruction of the Second World War followed almost immediately after the appearance of the book. After this holocaust, the structures of a technological and bureaucratic welfare state arose. It is safe to say that this society of ours is far removed from the reconstruction Mannheim hoped for. In a way, however, his call for reconstruction is still relevant, despite the fact that the socio-cultural and political scene has changed dramatically. The collapse of liberal democracy, the degeneration of individual liberty and the dictatorship of totalitarian regimes were very manifest phenomena in Mannheim's day. They were embodied in an "objective" manner in men like Hitler and Stalin, who from two entirely different backgrounds trampled on the most elementary human rights. The problems Mannheim and his contemporaries faced assumed many frightening dimensions, but they were at least "concrete" and clearly visible. Today we are confronted by quite similar problems, but we have somehow managed to wrap them in the comforts of economic abundance. Moreover, the concrete dimensions of the dehumanization in the thirties and forties have vanished into the abstract clouds of our supra-organized society. Each of us experiences forces of control in every fiber of his existence, but we hardly know the nature of this control and are therefore quite unable to defend our humanness.

Aware of his responsibility, Mannheim knew that a social scientist in those days could not stand by silently and just stick to the facts. One had to speak out, and Mannheim did so in a remarkably sober way. His main conclusion was that man in the age of reconstruction, which Mannheim thought to observe, had to evade both the ghostly ideology of liberalism and the temptation to follow dictators of one sort or the other. Man must learn, according to him, to live with planning, that is, with a rationally and intellectually directed organization of society, of man, and of human existence. Freedom as such is no longer possible; it has to be planned too. We have to learn to plan society or we are doomed to either total chaos or some form of totalitarianism.

Mannheim knew that such an approach had to transcend the limitations of empirical research in order to arrive at a theoretical interpretation and understanding of the nature and main trends of society. Sociological specialists have left the interpretation and assessment of modern culture to laymen for too long. "(T)his period of fact finding," Mannheim wrote, "has lasted long enough. We must try to create a period of theoretical integration that must be carried out with the same sense of responsibility which the specialists always feel in approaching their particular problems."[6]

Mannheim's study could be dismissed by saying it was written some thirty years ago. The socio-political scene has altered radically. The book has done its task. Why should we return to it? But things are not that simple. As everyone knows, the problem of democracy (i.e. of human freedom in a society with equal opportunities for all to realize their capacities) is still as much at stake today as it was in Mannheim's time. Perhaps even more so, since the very forces of planning and control, seen by Mannheim as the main factors in reconstruction, have resulted in a pluralistic, highly specialized, and differentiated society in which the individual easily loses all sense of reality, meaning and freedom. We must continue where Mannheim halted. His situation, moreover, was, as I said before, easier in that the dictatorial forces of his day were very concrete and manifest. Our situation is much more quixotic: we fight windmills that vanish the moment we try to attack them. This needs a new "diagnosis of our time."

There is one further consideration. Today, the basic problems of society are not essentially determined by the dilemma of democracy versus totalitarianism (or, geographically speaking, West versus East). These traditional lines of division and conflict are at bottom conditioned by traditional forms of nationalism and ethnocentrism. The fundamental dividing lines stem from the economic dilemma of affluence versus poverty (which largely parallels the "color line") and from the social dilemma of the individual versus industrial society and its forces of control and hierarchical power (which largely parallels the "generation gap"). This book will be limited mainly to a theoretical interpretation of the second dilemma. It focuses on the increasingly abstract nature of modern society and the forms of protest launched against it. Like the sorcerer's apprentice, modern man tries to regain control over the products of his social and cultural creativity. But, again like the sorcerer's apprentice, he often seems to lose his head. In such a situation, a new "diagnosis of our time" appears to be necessary. It might perhaps even contribute to the arrival of a society in which man is master again over a socio-cultural environment that he has created himself but that has reached momentarily an alarming stage of autonomy. Such a cultural analysis in the tradition of Mannheim strives for a philosophical interpretation and sociological analysis of the nature of abstract society and of the protests launched against it by modern men, particularly by those who have to live in it for the next four or five decades.

Theodor Geiger, whose *Demokratie ohne Dogma* (1950) offers a second starting point for our cultural analysis, was a convinced "positivist" who rejected traditional German idealism and its social philosophy. As a matter of fact, he was determined to debunk metaphysical ideologies of all sorts. This debunking was not, however, caused by some form of "scientistic nihilism," as is often the case with "positivists," but sprang from a fundamental sense of cultural responsibility. *Demokratie ohne Dogma* was his last book and summed up his critique of man in modern society. This society, he claimed, was more and more dominated by romantics who longed for intimate *Gemeinschaft*-like relations and complained about "mass society" with its atomization and alienation. The individual and his inner experiences were more and more pushed to the fore, while emotions and romantic experiences were opposed to the structures of modern society, which demands functions, not feelings. From expressionism in art to existentialism in philosophy, the "revolution of feelings" seized modern man. And because he did not feel happy, he scorned society—the big, amorphous mass society in which he no longer felt at home. Geiger then raised the intriguing question as to whether it was not man rather than society who was to be blamed for this. Was this not an adjustment fault on the part of modern man, Geiger asked, rather than a constructional fallacy in the constitution of modern society?

Geiger did not deny that modern mass society presented some genuine existential problems. He searched, as we will see later, for an answer in a renewed rationalism which allegedly could give back to man the power to cope with his socio-cultural environment. We will question the validity of this solution in the last chapter of this book. It suffices here to stress his clear insight into some of the most elementary processes of our time, namely individualism and emotionalism with their romantic intoxications. They have indeed determined the fifties and particularly the sixties to a great extent, and Geiger saw this at the end of the forties. Perhaps he went too far in his defense of modern society against its romantic critics. He was probably also too naïve in his interpretation of that society's bureaucratic technology. But he had a very crucial problem at hand, and his discussion of it has lost little of its actuality and urgency!

The two studies by Mannheim and Geiger suggest the kind of cultural analysis I am striving for in this book. Each period requires its own cultural analysis in which the signs of the time are gathered and interpreted. At the beginning of the seventies, in which the generations that were born after the Second World War and grew up in the affluence of a technological and bureaucratic society take the stage, a new cultural analysis as a contemporary "diagnosis of our time" seems to be mandatory. It was not so much courage or presumptuousness that drove me to the writing of this book as a growing uneasiness with the present situation of man in modern society, and in particular with man's reactions to this society. Needless to say, I see this interpretation as part of an ongoing discussion and not as the final analysis or the final answer.

I shall devote the remainder of this chapter to a brief outline of the main argument of the book. Chapter 2 provides the reader with an exposition of the theoretical framework in which all observations and interpretations concerning man in modern society will be placed and tested. Reduced to its essence, this framework consists of the sociological and philosophical theory of the homo duplex, i.e. of man as a double being: a unique individual with his own mode of existence and at the same time a member of a species, a social being who performs the roles that society has imposed on him. According to this theorem, which has been explored by as different people as Luther, and Durkheim, Simmel, Mead and Plessner, man has two points of gravity, within and outside himself—he is both *homo internus* and *homo externus*. From this simple statement stem several problems which we hope to discuss in this book. Since the theorem is used as the basic framework for our interpretation of man and modern society, we must elaborate on it in some detail. Its nature and development will be discussed under the heading "The Theoretical Stage."

After the theoretical basis for our discussion has thus been laid, we can proceed to investigate systematically three problems: (1) What is the nature of modern society's structure compared to pre-industrial societies? (2) What does this society do to the modern individual? (3) How does modern man react to it? The main conclusions can be summarized briefly in advance.

The structures of modern society, as we will see, have grown increasingly pluralistic and independent of man. Through an ever enlarging process of differentiation, modern society acquired a rather autonomous and abstract nature confronting the individual with strong but strange forms of control. It demands the attitudes of obedient functionaries from its inhabitants who experience its control as an unfamiliar kind of authority. That means societal control is no longer characterized by a familylike authority but dominated by bureaucratic neutrality and unresponsiveness. The individual often seems to be doomed to endure this situation passively, since the structures of society vanish in abstract air if he tries to grasp their very forces of control. No wonder that many seek refuge in one or another form of retreat. Some withdraw into the private spheres of life (e.g. the family, or the "gang") where they conform to society silently. Others reduce their humanity to the uncontrolled experiences and emotions of their inner life where they float away on "psychedelic" visions of sorts. Many retreat to a subculture or counterculture with its own life style not thwarted by the rules and regulations of "straight society." Conformistic privatization, gnostic subjectivism, and cultural anarchism are the forms of retreat that leave modern society for what it actually is. But there are also revolutionaries who protest against society in more or less violent forms of activism. The chapters on "Abstract Society" and "The Spirit of Protest" will cover these problems and discuss them in the frame of reference of the homo duplex theorem.

There are, however, two features of modern society that require special attention. As the discussion on abstract society will indicate, our time is characterized by the dilemma of an increasing autonomization of societal structures vis-à-vis an equally increasing autonomization of the modern individual. The chapter called "Autonomy in Pluralistic Society" will deal with this problem. In the second place, as men like Weber and Sombart have demonstrated, modern industrial society increases in rationality. The tremendous development of bureaucracy with its highly rational principle of efficiency is a very good illustration of this phenomenal process. Paradoxically, however, the modern individual seems to grow more and more irrational. The chapter on "Rationality and Irrationality" will be devoted to this issue.

Finally, seen in the light of the homo duplex theorem we can observe two reductions applied to the double nature of man: abstract society, on the one hand, reduces the modern individual to a social functionary (a one-sided *homo externus*) whereas this individual himself, on the other hand, exhibits the tendency to reduce his double nature into the opposite direction by either retreat or revolt, relying in both cases on irrational emotions and experiences, and longing for a social nirvana in which he can live as a "pure" individual without any form of institutional alienation (a one-sided *homo internus*).

The last chapter returns to the homo duplex theorem once more, but this time in a normative, socio-ethical application. That means, only as a double being, i.e. as an individual who is prepared to realize his Self within the "objectivity" and alienation of institutional structures and who refuses to surrender his rationality to the short-term shocks of his emotionality, is man going to survive in modern society in a *human* way. It is in this perspective that the modern spirit of protest is criticized, without, however, surrendering to the easy solutions of conformism. The sixties have made it abundantly clear that the forces of dehumanization originate in the autonomization of abstract society as well as in the romantic longings of the modern *homo internus*. This decade, it seems to me, represents a period of transition from the holocaust of two world wars to a world in which affluence and poverty, peace and war, overproduction and scarcity, consumption and starvation, the search for total freedom and the longing for totalitarian authority, set up a world-wide stage on which we and future generations will have to perform our roles. A diagnosis of this decade is necessary and might be fruitful. The present discussion is to be understood as a contribution to such an enterprise.

NOTES

1. Max Scheler, *Die Stellung des Menschen im Kosmos*, 1928 (Bern: Francke Verlag, 1962), transl. as *Man's Place in Nature* by H. Meyerhoff (New York: The Noonday Press, 1962).
2. Translation: "I revolt, therefore we are." Albert Camus, *L'Homme Révolté* (Paris: Gallimard, 1951), p. 36. The alternative use of "I" and "we" in this sentence is quite typical for our age!
3. Cf. Georg Simmel, *Soziologie* (Berlin: Duncker & Humblot, 1958[4]), p. 20. See also N. Spykman, *The Social Theory of Georg Simmel*, 1925 (New York: Atherton Press, 1966), p. 56. This book presents a very good survey of Simmel's social thought and is structured according to a tripartite division: methodology—sociology—social philosophy.
4. Karl Mannheim, *Man and Society in an Age of Reconstruction*, 1940 (London: Routledge & Kegan Paul, 1960).
5. Theodor Geiger, *Demokratie ohne Dogma*, 1950 (Muenchen: Szczesny Verlag, 1960). See also his *Arbeiten zur Soziologie*, ed. P. Trappe (Neuwied-Berlin: Luchterhand Verlag, 1962).
6. Karl Mannheim, *o.c.*, p. 31.

2

THE THEORETICAL STAGE

Man is a double being. He is a unique individual with his own mode of existence, his own thoughts and emotions, his own experiences of love, anxiety and loneliness, his own awareness of reality, and with his own body. My experience of life within the floating time structure of past, present and future cannot be experienced by anyone else.

But man is at the same time a member of a species, a social being who plays predefined social roles which urge him to think and act and feel according to the rules and patterns of his society. That means my unique experience of life is simultaneously a learned experience of a social life within the traditional structures of the "objective" time of clock and calendar.[1]

In this relatively simple proposition are embodied both the basic existential problems of man in society and the theoretical core problem of the social sciences which try to analyze and interpret man's social life.

Human ambiguity has always been a central issue in philosophy.[2] The subject-object dichotomy, for instance, kept human thinking in its grip from ancient Greek philosophy to modern epistemology. However, when man becomes conscious of social reality as a conditioning force, this ambiguity gains still another dimension. I shall limit myself to this social dimension of man's double nature.

It was not the modern sociologist who discovered man's social ambiguity. Long before the social sciences were established as a rational explanation of man's social life, individual thinkers were struck by the fact that man is simultaneously unique and socially predictable, free yet socially conditioned, a producer and a social product, a being who creates and plays roles.

As long as man experiences himself as an inherent part of

his social cosmos, the notion of ambiguity will hardly occur to him. Totemistic clans, the Greek polis, or feudal Europe, present themselves as all-embracing unities of which the individual constitutes an inseparable part. It is only when these organic unities collapse that man becomes aware of his individuality and partial uniqueness. Consequently we might then expect philosophical theories emerging on the double nature of man. Not amazingly, Martin Luther was one of the first in Western civilization to be aware of this anthropological dichotomy of man as subject and object, as unique individual and general social being. Interestingly enough, he was also one of the first to profess that man's authenticity lies in the subjective and individual part of his being. This notion, as we will see, has prevailed throughout the modern world until this very day. Naturally, Luther discussed his theory on the double nature of man within the theological frame of reference of his time.

Luther distinguished two realms and three estates when speaking about his society. Through the three constitutive spheres of medieval life, the estates of family, church and state, runs a division of worldly and spiritual realms. This means that in the family as well as in the church or the state, one lives simultaneously as an officially conditioned person, playing the roles of the worldly realm, and as a free individual, dependent on nobody but God who rules over the spiritual and worldly realms. Taking himself and the royal ruler of his state as example, Luther wrote: "I said time and again that one should distinguish official function and personality. These are totally different human beings, the ones who are called Hans or Martin and those who are called elector or Doctor and preacher."[3] He then formulates (again, in theological terms, of course) the double nature of man: "Each individual human being has on earth two personalities: one for himself, bound to nobody but God alone, but also a worldly personality, through which he is bound to other people."[4]

Thus in the main institutional sectors of medieval society (family, church, and state) man lives, as Luther formulated it, as *homo internus* and as *homo externus*, the former being the free, religious man, the latter the socially conditioned man. In other words, Luther saw the true realm of freedom only outside of society and its institutional relationships.

One must realize that Luther's *homo internus* of the spiritual realm was essentially *homo religiosus,* namely a free Christian. Luther confined man's freedom and his religiosity to the inner world of experiences. This became the main root for all of German pietism and its secularized brother, romanticism. *Homo internus,* trapped in the aimless and passive abodes of his inner life, is opposed to *homo externus* and his social dependence. He is the "man for himself" as we encounter him from the end of the Middle Ages until today in many disguises. Indeed, after Luther it is only a small step to define *homo internus* as authentic and to oppose him to *homo externus* as his alienated brother.

Another consideration must be added. Luther's *homo internus* is essentially free from social responsibility. He is responsible to God alone, but when the God concept is secularized he will easily become self-centered and ego-directed. Responsibility is then left to *homo externus* and bears the stigma of inauthenticity and alienation which easily result in abdication of responsibility. This again is a trend we can observe from Luther to this very day.

It is not surprising to find Ludwig Feuerbach as the next important analyst of man's social ambiguity. After all, Feuerbach was a German theologian. He made an important step, however, by placing the problem in a non-theological, anthropological framework. In opposition to Hegel's idealism, Feuerbach chose the "material," bodily man as the basis for his anthropology. Marx in his famous *Theses on Feuerbach* (1845) admired him for this materialism, but severely criticized his determinism. Sensual reality to Feuerbach means "objective reality" passively experienced by man through his senses. He speaks about reality as if it were an inert objectivity which imposes itself on man and is experienced by him in a passive and subjective way. Marx rejected this dualism which opposes to subjective passive man an overwhelming objective reality. To Marx, man is not an aesthetic, passively experiencing being. His nature is characterized by praxis, and the reality he confronts is his own product. Thus Marx's *Theses on Feuerbach* contain a sharp critique of all forms of

subjectivism and aestheticism that confine man's authenticity
to the inner world of experiences and emotions.

Feuerbach also advanced the so-called *altruistic principle,*
meant not as an ethical but as an anthropological category.
Man, according to this principle, is a being who depends on
his fellow men. The "I" cannot exist without a "you." Life,
that is, corporeality, sexuality, love, language, interaction
and even contacts with things and animals, is impossible without a fellow man. Only through a non-I, through someone
else, does life become understandable and meaningful. This
principle continued to dominate all discussions on intentionality and intersubjectivity, from Dilthey, Husserl, Mead and
Buber to Schutz, Buytendijk, Sartre and Plessner.[5]

But the discussion of the generic relation between the "I"
and the "you" soon appears to be limited if the "you" is not
enlarged into "the others," i.e. the community or the group
or society. It has to be interpreted in terms of a "generalized
other" (G. H. Mead) as a typified player of predefined roles.
This enlargement of Feuerbach's altruistic principle was undertaken by modern sociology and social psychology, notedly
by C. H. Cooley, W. I. Thomas, G. H. Mead, Georg Simmel
and Émile Durkheim. Their endeavors led to modern role
theory where the social ambiguity of man found its final
theoretical exploration. On this point there is a remarkable
convergence of American and European social thought.

William James's pragmatism is an important souce for all
social thought on the ambiguity of man in society. To James,
human consciousness is not so much an entity as a process,
an ongoing stream of thought and subjective life. Its main
quality is the awareness man can have of himself. Thus, a
person appears in two ways: "partly known, partly knower,
partly object and partly subject." He called the known, "objective" part the "me" and the knowing, "subjective" part the
"I." The "me" is everything a person has knowledge and
awareness of. It consists of three parts, the *material me* (the
body and everything related to physical existence, such as
clothes, houses, possessions, etc.), the *social me* (the part of
one's self that is recognized by others and upon which they
base their image of me), and the *spiritual me* (the state of
consciousness and all psychic facilities).

The "I" is the ability to experience and to be aware. It experiences the outer world as well as its own "me." The "I" is not an entity (as the Hegelian spirit often seems to be) but an ongoing process, a happening.

C. H. Cooley applied the Jamesian approach to the social sciences but reduced them to psychology by claiming that society was merely made up of peoples' imaginations of one another. Society is the name for mental phenomena, for ideas people have of each other represented by symbols and names. In this framework, he developed his well-known theory of the looking-glass self, which claims that man's self comes about when he reacts to the opinions others have of him. Like Feuerbach's altruistic principle, this theory holds that man's personality and individuality can develop only through contacts with others. Although caught in psychological notions, it clearly attempts to transcend the solipsism of the *homo internus* notion.

Like Cooley, W. I. Thomas centered his analyses around the individual and his attitudes rather than institutional structures and their functions. Such an attitudinal approach needs a methodological warning. Indeed, Thomas stressed repeatedly that the natural and social environment of man is the environment as he (i.e. this man living in this situation) experiences and sees it and *not* the environment as the social scientist sees it: ". . . the environment by which he is influenced and to which he adapts himself, is *his* world, not the objective world of science—is nature and society as he sees them, not as the scientist sees them."[6] For that very reason, any analysis of social reality is far from exhausted by an interpretation of the formal organization of this reality (its institutional structures and their functions). One has rather to penetrate into the subjectively imposed and experienced meanings of the individual living within these structures: "A social institution can be fully understood only if we do not limit ourselves to the abstract study of its formal organization, but analyze the way in which it appears in the personal experience of various members of the group and follow the influence which it has upon their lives."[7]

Thomas sees social life (also called "social becoming" or "social evolution") as being determined by an intrinsic relationship between social organization (or the objective reality of institutions) and individual consciousness. This interdependence has consequences for man's personality: he appears as a double being, producer and product alike: "The human personality is both a continually producing factor and a continually produced result of social evolution, and this double relation expresses itself in every elementary social fact. Personal evolution is always a struggle between the individual and society—a struggle for self-expression on the part of the individual, for his subjection on the part of society—and it is in the total course of this struggle that the personality—not as a static 'essence' but as a dynamic, continually evolving set of activities—manifests and constructs itself."[8]

We can therefore no longer speak about man and society in one-sided terms. Social reality does not "make" the individual, nor does the individual "construct" social reality, but both statements are true simultaneously. The individual can admittedly develop only under the influence of his sociocultural environment, but this environment is changed in its turn during the development of the individual. Thomas adds to this: "His influence upon the environment may be scarcely noticeable socially, may have little importance for others, but it is important to himself, since, as we have said, the world in which he lives is not the world as society or the scientific observer sees it but as he sees it himself."[9]

Thus, to Thomas, social psychology is primarily the study of *individual attitudes* which are directed toward and influenced by a socio-cultural environment. An individual attitude may be defined roughly as a process within the human organism that causes action in the social world. Attitudes are, for example, hunger that drives someone to acquiring food and to eating it; the poet's inspiration that leads him to writing; the fear and devotion of the believer that become manifest in cults and rituals.[10] These attitudes have their counterparts in *social values*, defined by Thomas as objects in society that are accessible to the members and endowed with a particular meaning. Examples are the food we eat, the poems we read, the religious myths and doctrines we believe. As such, empirical objects are value-less if they do not contain a specific meaning for our social actions. A piece of timber is just an inert natural object, but a wooden chair represents a social value since it has meaning in our daily activities. This means that the meaning of social values is inherent in the course of social action.

Social values and individual attitudes are connected by human activity. Attitudes cause action, and this action gives meaning to the world of objects, making them into social values. Feelings and impressions (attitudes) cause the poet to write poetry. Reading and reciting these poems transform the words and sentences into social values.[11] We see clearly here how Thomas tried to express the social ambiguity of man: his meaningful environment is human and his personality is dependent on this meaningful social environment.

If we put these attitudes under closer scrutiny, Thomas claims, we will discover that they are grouped together. Organized groups of attitudes develop according to patterns. Some of these become so predominant that one can construct "types of personality." But before we consider Thomas' typology of personalities, we must pay attention to his distinction between *temperament* and *character*.

These are two different groups of attitudes which each in its own way determines man's personality. The group of attitudes called temperament is fundamental and original in that it exists independently of any social influence. It is comprised, roughly, of man's basic drives and instincts, determined biologically rather than socially. Hunger, for instance, is an attitude of the temperamental group. Sex is another. Character, on the other hand, is a highly organized group of interrelated attitudes that are not instinctive but intellectual. Temperamental attitudes are directed almost exclusively toward natural objects devoid of meaning. They are conditioned by their sensual contents. The character attitudes draw a sharp line between biological and social life. A man, one could say, lives on the temperamental level only if he places himself outside the context of social meaning: "In the face of the world of social meanings he stands powerless; he is not even conscious of the existence of this reality, and when the latter manifests itself to him in changes of the material reality upon which his instincts bear, *he is quite lost and either passively submits to the unexpected, or aimlessly revolts*. Such is the position of the animal or the infant in human society"[12] (italics mine).

In only a few words, Thomas thus formulated the main argument of the present book. <u>If man places himself outside the meanings of social life,</u> he reduces his nature to that of <u>a conditioned animal or of an infant. As a result, he is unable to act adequately if changes in</u> his environment occur. Instead, he stares at his surroundings passively and either submits to the unexpected or revolts aimlessly against it. As I shall argue later, this seems to happen to modern man in our abstract society: as a conformist he submits to the unexpected, as a protester he often appears to be aimless. Indeed, contemporary man has more temperament than character.

As a social psychologist, Thomas was mainly interested in the attitudes linked to social reality. Living and acting in society, he claimed, man has to construct a life organization. He cannot just act at random but must organize his activities within a stable and structured order. Together with the desire for new experiences, man possesses a strong desire for stability. This stability can be natural (biological) or social. Natural stability is established by habituation. Habits are part of biological temperaments and the result of "the tendency to repeat the same act in similar material conditions."[13] As such, habitual stability depends on similar natural situations. Social stability, on the other hand, is located on the conscious level of rationality. It cannot depend on similar situations, because social situations are never similar. If they are similar, it is because they have been defined as such by the individual: "And this is what society expects him to do when it requires of him a stable life-organization; it does not want him to react instinctively in the same way to the same material conditions, but to construct reflectively similar social situations even if material conditions vary. The uniformity of behavior it tends to impose upon the individual is not a uniformity of organic habits but of consciously followed rules."[14]

Each individual develops "general schemes of situations"[15] which guarantee the necessary stability for his actions. The way in which these schemes are constructed depends naturally on the character (i.e. the group of conscious attitudes) of the individual. At this point, Thomas introduces his typology of <u>three main characters, the Philistine, the Bohemian, and the Creative Man.</u> This typology will prove to be of the utmost importance to the main argument of my book.

The Philistine is reluctant to allow many new social influences into his attitudes. His character has reached a degree of stability that leaves him open to only a limited number of influences. He is a conservative conformist whose general scheme of situations depends pretty much on the status quo that was reached once upon a time in his life. His is an "over-adjusted type" of personality, accepting the prevailing definitions, values and norms. His first and foremost interest is security, even if he has to sacrifice his own individuality for it. The Bohemian, on the contrary, is reluctant to adjust to any situation and will always try to escape the rules and norms of society. He does so at the cost of a stable formation of his character, mainly because he stays open to all kinds of influences. His is an "unadjusted" chaotic personality type—not settled down, always on the move.

The Philistine and the Bohemian, we could say, represent two opposite types. In the former the social aspects dominate individuality, whereas in the latter individual aspects prevail and prevent the stability that only society can offer him.

The third type, Creative Man, represents the social ambiguity of man in an ideal way. His "character is settled and organized, but involves the possibility and even necessity of evolution."[16] He is driven by the desire for new experiences, he redefines situations (i.e. he creates new reality), and he renovates norms and social values. Creative Man is not an absolutist who restlessly reaches for the best and the ultimate, but he is a renovator and creator within the parameters of societal institutions. He is, therefore, neither a retreatist nor a conformist, nor a revolutionist.

One will hardly meet a personality in everyday life that represents one of these types in ideal form. They are constructed ideal types. Many Bohemians, as a matter of fact, are often rather philistine; many Philistines are plagued by bohemian desires. These types make a model which expresses in a cogent way the social ambiguity of man. It is a theoretical reconstruction of the nature of man in an institutional environment.

The social psychology of George Herbert Mead is an even greater attempt to explain man's social ambiguity. In an unprecedented way, Mead manages in his *Mind, Self and Society* (1934) to analyze man and society in such a way that social structure and individual experience are brought together in one single focus.

Mead saw himself as a behaviorist but rejected the basic tenet of Watsonian behaviorism according to which such inner realities as "experience" and "consciousness" are to be excluded from scientific psychology. Watson did not deny the existence of "mind" and "psyche" but believed they could be understood only by means of introspection. And since introspection is more an aesthetic than a scientific method of analysis, he felt it should be avoided by the psychologist. The only observable reality the psychologist can deal with is outward and conditioned behavior. Thus, man can be studied scientifically only on the level of Pavlov's salivating dog, which means that behavior is only what the scientist sees and measures "objectively." This principle, as we saw before, was rejected by Thomas. Mead rejected it too.

In Mead's social behaviorism, experiences and attitudes, mind and consciousness, are viewed as inseparable components of one process: human behavior. Mind and self as inherent parts of behavior are not studied mystically through introspection but subjected to a scientific analysis. Mead proposed the concept of *gesture* as the main target for such a scientific analysis. Following certain notions of Darwin and Wundt, he viewed the gesture as a transition from the inner processes of psychic life to the outside event of human action. Gestures are partly conscious and partly unconscious, partly attitude and partly action, partly "inside" and partly "outside." They are, simultaneously, the beginning of communication and the source for all interaction.

Many psychologists, Mead said, make the serious mistake of considering emotions and consciousness, roughly speaking the "human psyche," as "something there," existing in man's inner world *prior to* any behavior. Mead's social psychology is one great attempt to prove that it is the other way around:

human psyche and consciousness occur in social interaction and are the result rather than the cause of behavior. This has often been misunderstood as a theory on the origin of mind and self. Rather than analyzing the birth of mind and self, Mead tries to develop a theory of the *evolution of mind and self*, given the process of interaction. To have interaction (co-operation) at all, the human species admittedly depends on a higher physiological development of the central nervous system. But at the moment that interaction and language occur, man's mind and self can develop to the degree that they have. Not the central nervous system, but the interaction among men is the determining factor in the evolution of mind and self.

The gesture functions as the bridge between outside social behavior and inner psychic life. Darwin had already pointed out that gestures, as beginnings of acts, arouse emotional responses in others. If a dog makes gestures of an attack, another dog will respond immediately and express aggressiveness. The human face in particular is a field of emotional expressions and vague beginnings of acts.[17] Darwin, however, interpreted consciousness as a state of inner life prior to any behavior. Mead rejected that: "We are rather forced to conclude that consciousness is an emergent from such behavior; that so far from being a precondition of the social act, the social act is a precondition of it."[18]

In Mead's theory, the gesture expresses the social ambiguity of man. It is a stimulus for a response on the part of another actor, which in its turn stimulates a response on the part of the first actor. For example, if someone swings his fist under your nose with an angry expression on his face, you react immediately (that is, without reflection). You step back and assume an attitude of defense. This response has a feedback effect and will in its turn act as stimulus for the other. He may withdraw, in which case the interaction process remains abortive. But if he attacks, a full-grown interaction, called "fight," will develop. It all started with a conversation of gestures, going back and forth between the participants, probably accompanied by growls and other vocal gestures. It ends with real interaction, like a fight or violent shouting and calling names or an angry but polite conversation. In other words, there is a triadic relationship between an original gesture, its adjustive response and the resulting social act initiated by the gesture and its response. The crucial point in this sequence is the response to the initial gesture. If this response has the same "content" as the initial gesture (i.e. if the response reinforces the original gesture), we get the beginning of meaningful and symbolic interaction. From this we can draw the conclusion that the meaning of our behavior and our understanding of it are not prior to any interaction but occur as processes within this interaction itself!

This whole triadic relationship of gesture, adjustive response, and complete interaction, is, however, internalized by the individuals participating in the exchange. We address ourselves as others address us. We put ourselves in the place of the other and act toward ourselves as if we were the other. In other words, I can understand the response of the other to my initial gesture only if I address this gesture also to myself, treating myself as if I were the other. In the same way the other's response is addressed to an internalized other within myself. Only by *taking the role of the other* are we able to understand the conversation of gestures and the resulting interaction or linguistic communication. And through this internalization (i.e. by taking the role of the other) man becomes self-conscious and develops his personality. Again, the self is not something inborn in man, prior to social behavior; it is not an entity to be conceived of in spatial terms (like, for instance, Freud's division of the psyche in three "floors": the ego in between superego and id), but arises during man's interaction in which he takes the role of others. In giving someone directions as to how to proceed to a certain street, we make sense to the other only if we internalize his role of listener and address ourselves as if we were the other.[19] If in talking to another we do not internalize his role as listener, the other is liable to say, "It doesn't make sense to me." It happens quite often that we are then compelled to say more or less embarrassedly, "Actually I don't understand it myself either."

At this point, Mead, following James, introduces the distinction between the "I" and the "me" in the self. Formulated briefly, we might see the "I" as the capacity to take the role of the other and the psychic component in man that internalizes the interaction process. The "me" is then the internalized other itself. The others around me have attitudes toward my acting and speaking. I internalize these attitudes into my self and react toward them. In other words, I internalize the attitudes of many others and these internalizations constitute what is social in me. I react to these internalizations when I react to others in my daily activities: "The 'I' is the response of the organism to the attitudes of the others; the 'me' is the organized set of attitudes of others which one himself assumes. The attitudes of the others constitute this organized 'me' and then one reacts toward that as an 'I.'"[20]

As the last quote indicates, the attitudes of the others show distinct similarities, like Thomas' "scheme of situations". Groups of people in certain situations tend to respond to gestures in similar and predictable ways. If you swing your fist under the nose of a police officer you know in advance (and pretty accurately) how he is going to react. You have already internalized the response before you perform the gesture. There are many such organized forms of behavior which are collective and organized attitudes. Mead calls them *institutions*. This means that besides a relatively small group of significant others (parents, children, spouse, friends) a large group of generalized others with typical roles (teacher, police officer, student, preacher, worker, etc.) is being internalized by us in our daily round of activities. The "me" consists mainly of the generalized attitudes that have been internalized by the "I." The "me" is society in man, and it bears the structured organization that characterizes the institutions of society.

From this, Mead draws a conclusion that is very important for the main argument of this book. Society and its institutions are indispensable for the development and the meaningful coherence of mind and self, intelligence and personality. The institutions are a condition for genuinely human life: ". . . without social institutions of some sort, without the organized social attitudes and activities by which social institutions are constituted, there could be no fully mature individual selves or personalities at all; for the individuals involved in the general social life-process of which social institutions are organized manifestations can develop and possess fully mature selves or personalities only in so far as each of them reflects or prehends in his individual experience these organized social attitudes and activities which social institutions embody or represent."[21] In sum, social ambiguity is a human condition since the personality of man is developed to its full potentialities only if the "I" is confronted by a socially organized "me." The "me" as the institutional part of the self is therefore not the alienated counterpart of a pure "I" but the very field of expression on which the "I" depends.

It is, at this point, important to discuss the very difficult question of what precisely the "I" component of the self is. Is it a part of the human psyche that exists prior to any interaction?

It is actually impossible, according to Mead, to speak about the "I": "The 'I' does not get into the limelight; we talk to ourselves but we do not see ourselves. The 'I' reacts to the self which arises through the taking of the attitudes of others. Through taking those attitudes we have introduced the 'me' and we react to it as an 'I.'"[22] Amazingly enough, the "I" is here almost separated from the self as a kind of a priori psychological reality. It is pure actuality and cannot be caught in any reflection: *The 'I' of this moment is present in the 'me' of the next moment.* There again I cannot turn around quick enough to catch myself."[23] The "I" is the pure experience which flows into the "me" the next moment. I can remember that I reacted to the "me" a second ago, but at the very moment that this memory occurs the "I" is already part of the "me." In other words, the "I" is what the French philosopher Henri Bergson has called *durée*, the pure time awareness that becomes "objective" in past time.

The "I" and the "me" do not always remain separated but can fuse into each other. This fusion, which causes a sense of exaltation, is found most clearly in religious and patriotic experiences. It is the feeling that one's interest is the interest of all, that everyone is at one with each other, that one's individuality is embedded in the collectivity of the community. It is the experience of a *unio mystica* in which the "I" evaporates into the "me" and the "me" is experienced as one cosmic "I."[24] It is in this kind of mystical *Gemeinschaft,* we might add, that man transcends his ambiguity. As we will see in the next chapter, the primitive in his totemistic clan or the individual in the medieval Corpus Christianum were much nearer to this fusion of the "I" and the "me" than modern man in abstract industrial society ever can be. The latter faces a growingly autonomous and differentiated society and experiences his "me" as the alienated part of his personality. Consequently he indulges in the romantic desires of his anti-institutional mood, which poses the pure "I" as the essence of his existence. This is a subjectivism that claims that absolute freedom, ultimate meaning and utter reality can be found in an annihilation of the "me" and the aggrandizement of the "I." To Mead, this would entail the destruction of all communication and thus the destruction of mind, self and meaning. We must come back to this point at a later stage of our discussion.

Readers who are acquainted with the different sociological schools may object to the preceding survey of various theories on man's social ambiguity, claiming that I have remained almost exclusively in the field of social psychology and asking whether this problem has any relevance for a more structural approach in sociology. Rather than exploring the theories of social ambiguity within the framework of structural functionalism, which is beyond the scope of this book, I shall restrict myself to a brief discussion of the father of all sociological structuralism, Émile Durkheim.

Durkheim, as is well known, tried to save sociology from the threat of psychological reduction by stressing the objectivity of social institutions, which he usually called "social facts." As a sociologist one should consider social facts as things existing prior to and outside of individual man and individual experiences. Their most conspicuous quality is a coercive power which keeps society from disintegrating into anomie. This coercion gains momentum by man's internalization of these social facts through the process of education (i.e. socialization). Education, says Durkheim, molds the child into a social and mature being who will act and think in accordance with the traditional ways of life as they are embedded in the social institutions. Because of this, man can be called a *homo duplex,* a double being: ". . . man is double. There are two beings in him: an individual being which has its foundation in the organism and the circle of whose activities is therefore strictly limited, and a social being which represents the highest reality in the intellectual and moral order that we can know by observation—I mean society. . . . In so far as he belongs to society, the individual transcends himself, both when he thinks and when he acts."[25]

Although there is, according to Durkheim, "something impersonal in us because there is something social in all of us," it is society and the social being in us that give our lives stability, certainty and the higher reality of a moral order. To Durkheim, society is the storehouse of truth and morality, an essential condition for human life.

It often seems as if Durkheim restricted the "individual part" of homo duplex to the physiological aspect of the human organism in order to proclaim the "social part" as the realm of freedom and morality. This leads to a strange paradox since the "social being" in man seems to consist of internalized social coercion. Indeed, Durkheim's "individual being" lacks too many of the qualities of Mead's "I" to give a balanced picture of homo duplex.

The Durkheimian view of man and society, as has often been remarked, carries the dangers of determinism, which becomes particularly clear if one confronts this view with a Marxian perspective. Durkheim, incidentally, was in many ways a typical representative of the *fin de siècle* bourgeois society in France. Since he was of Jewish background, he must have encountered some resistance on his path of socialization into the social establishment of his days, the days of the infamous Dreyfus affair. One could accuse this society in anger, as Émile Zola did, but one could also sublimate one's anger and frustration theoretically by eulogizing it on a general and abstract level, as Émile Durkheim did. It seems safe to assert that Durkheim failed to pay sufficient attention to the forces of *alienation* implied in all forms of societal coercion. As a matter of fact, Durkheim was not concerned with alienation as the decline of human freedom and individuality, but with anomie as the threat of social disintegration and chaos. In this respect, he was the precise opposite of Karl Marx.

To Marx, the source of all alienation lies in the division of labor, which in turn is the origin of all institutionalization. Division of labor transforms human production and creativity into fragmented tasks. As a result one is no longer free to produce in a creative and human way, but has to fulfill the requirements of a specific job. Thus, the producer is estranged from his own creativity. Moreover, the economic process of buying and selling adds to this estrangement the alienation of the producer from his product. The product is no longer an expression of creativity but a commodity to be bought and sold. This leads to still another alienation, the alienation between human beings because some of them profit from these commodities and others (tragically those who produced them) are exploited for the sake of this very profit. In the final capitalistic stage of this dehumanizing development, the producers of commodities, i.e. the workers, have become commodities themselves—bearers of productive working power to be bought and sold by the capitalist on the labor market. The proletariat represents the last possible stage of alienation: deprived of all qualities and possessions (even of their tools, namely the means of production), the proletarians in capitalist society are stripped of all human characteristics and reduced to profitable things. Social coercion has become sheer oppression and dehumanization.

According to Marx's anthropology, man's nature is characterized by his production as the expression of what he called *praxis*. Through division of labor, however, certain processes of production develop which acquire a momentum of their own and grow into thinglike structures. These are not "natural" realities but historical constructions. It is an act of reification and false consciousness to conceive of the institutions of bourgeois capitalist society as "natural" or "God given" structures. They are not "natural," and if they dehumanize, man is able to overthrow them in a revolution. The institutions of capitalist society, beginning with its class structure, are dehumanizing fetters which coerce man's praxis and incapacitate his creativity and freedom. Only a classless society which does away with such structural fetters as the state, the church and the family, can bring back to man his freedom and genuinely human creativity. Thus in the Marxian dream of a classless society there are no institutions and thus no alienation and dehumanization. The communist community consists of human beings who play and produce without being coerced by institutional fetters and the greed of private property.

After the communist community has been restored (it is a restoration of a mythological paradise), man will no longer be double as producer and product, as individual and class member. He will regain his true and creative nature, experiencing his environment as a community in which he feels at home at last. It will be the end of history.

Sociologically speaking, Marx tried to think the unthinkable. He yearned for a society without institutions, for human praxis without limiting structures, freedom without alienation, human action without institutional rules and norms. In the final analysis, Marx did not protest against simply capitalism and bourgeois society. He rejected any form of society and societal control. He longed for pure and absolute praxis. He wanted the end of man's social ambiguity. In Marx we encounter at bottom a romantic and gnostic revolt against the social condition of man.[26]

Georg Simmel managed to evade the one-sidedness of either Durkheim, who overemphasized the importance of institutions, or Marx, who revolted against them. He envisaged man's position in society as moving between two extremes on a continuum: man can sacrifice his personality in a relationship of love (as with friends and lovers), or he transcends himself in devotion to a vocation (as in the case of the Roman Catholic priest). In both cases, man's individuality has been transcended into a transindividual reality through which the awareness of individuality has actually increased. Or, in the terms of Mead, the "I" has merged with the "me," which causes the exalted experience of transindividuality. The opposite pole of the continuum, according to Simmel, is man's situation in modern society with all its efficiency and bureaucracy. Here the individual separates himself from the roles he is playing: "Except in the highest leading positions, the individual life and the tone of the total personality is removed from the social action. Individuals are merely engaged in an exchange of performance and counter-performance that takes place according to objective norms."[27] Simmel then formulated his notion of social ambiguity: "A society is, therefore, a structure which consists of beings who stand inside and outside of it at the same time. This fact forms the basis for one of the most important sociological phenomena, namely, that between a society and its component individuals a relation may exist as if between two parties. . . . The individual can never stay within a unit which he does not at the same time stay outside of, he is not incorporated into any order without also confronting it."[28] This dual position of man, i.e. the "within" and "without" relation between man and society, contains a "synthesis or simultaneity of two logically contradictory characterizations of man."[29] This means that man is *simultaneously* a unique autonomous individual and a player of generalized roles. One can compare this, according to Simmel, with the seeming contradiction inherent in the causality concept: it contains the two opposite principles of cause and effect. Similarly, all social life is characterized by the social and the individual, the general and the unique.

In his discussion of social ambiguity Simmel introduced the notion of role playing, which has become a very useful analytical tool in contemporary sociological theory. There is not space to engage here in a detailed discussion of *modern role theory*. I shall limit myself instead to two European theorists who dealt with this issue in a way that is relevant to the main argument of this book.

Ralf Dahrendorf, one of the leading contemporary European sociologists, wrote an essay on role theory, *Homo Sociologicus*,[30] in which he discusses the paradox that man, as he is experienced in everyday life, appears to be different from the artificial man as he is analyzed and interpreted by the social scientist. Total man, as he is experienced, cannot be grasped by the social scientist, who constructs an artificial creature that blindly obeys the rules and laws laid down by the social scientist in his theoretical model. Total man is thus divided by various social scientists into *homo economicus,* who fits the model of the economist and acts according to economic laws, *homo psychologicus,* who is part of the psychologist's model and obeys his causal laws, *homo sociologicus*, who belongs to a sociological model and acts in accordance with the laws established therein, and so on in all the social sciences. Homo economicus, homo psychologicus, homo sociologicus are not real human beings of flesh and blood but the types and puppets of scientific models.

But—and at this point Dahrendorf steps from model to reality—if we look at social reality carefully enough, we will observe real human beings who are compelled to play predefined social roles in a very typified way. As a matter of fact, we cannot take a single step without encountering society as what Dahrendorf called "an irritating fact." This means that the sociological model of homo sociologicus with all its (artificial) causality is real to a considerable degree! Total man in social reality seems to be homo sociologicus indeed—a puppet conforming to the rules of society and performing the roles imposed on him by society. There seems to be very little freedom left. The methodological model, in other words, becomes real and presents a *moral dilemma:* the nightmare of overadjusted, social man.

Several European social scientists (among them F. Tenbruck, H. Schelsky, A. Gehlen, and H. Plessner[31]) have criticized Dahrendorf for this transition from model to reality and have called it an illegitimate one. Allegedly, Dahrendorf reified a scientific model, which is necessarily artificial and dominated by mere causality and rationality. For sociology as an analytic and value-free discipline, there are no moral problems whatsoever. Morality is involved only when man has the freedom to perform certain actions and is able to judge them according to his values. Both this freedom and these values are absent in sociological models where only causality and rationality rule. Indeed, Dahrendorf does not distinguish between two logically different kinds of homo sociologicus: one in the methodological frame of reference, who is an artificial construction of the social scientist, the other on the level of everyday existence, who is a role player and as such conditioned by the forces of social coercion. Only the latter can pose a moral dilemma, because only he can be the bearer of human freedom and moral values. It is this everyday man who confronts us with the dilemma of homo duplex, simultaneously free and conditioned, unique and typified. This seems particularly true of modern man in a pluralistic, abstract society. In sum, Dahrendorf may be wrong in his reification of the homo sociologicus model, but he has opened our eyes to the moral dilemma of man as a double being, a creative individual who is in danger of being alienated by his other part, the social role player.

The German philosopher and sociologist Helmuth Plessner took up the discussion on alienation and social roles and presented some ideas that are relevant to our argument. The role concept is important to him because it points at the social framework in which the individual performs socially relevant movements. It catches, as it were, the individual person as well as the social system of institutions in which he acts. It therefore formulates very clearly the fundamental ambiguity of man extended between two poles, the private and the official (i.e. the social). Plessner calls this ambiguity man's *Doppelgaengertum*,[32] that is, his essential nature as a double being.

To Plessner, the main fallacies of both existentialism and Marxism lie in the belief that man's social part is an alienation of his "true Self," which is believed to be situated in the private and/or inner spheres of man. Plessner, who always stressed man's *excentricity* (i.e. the fact that man's main point of gravity lies outside his self), offers a valuable alternative to these Marxist and existentialist reductions of homo duplex and their common ideology of alienation. In order to be genuinely human, Plessner asserts, *man needs the duplication of his self in the form of social roles which are originally not part of this self.* Man is only man if he duplicates himself in "alien" roles and tries to identify himself with these roles. His "true self" or "true identity" is not "something" that is left after his social roles have been stripped off, but can be established only through the individual's act of identification with his roles. It is romanticism (going back as far as Luther's *homo internus*) to defend the individual and his inner or private experiences against the alleged alienation of an "irritating fact, called society" (Dahrendorf), just as it is romanticism to search for reality, meaning and freedom within man's inner subjective life.

Freedom, to quote Arnold Gehlen, who is in accordance with Plessner on this point, can be realized only through the alienation imposed on us by society and its institutional demands.[33] The same holds true for our identity. Whether we like it or not, our true identity remains extended between two poles, the individual and the social, the unique and the common. Man's social ambiguity is an inescapable fate.

The survey I have tried to give here of some of the main theories of man's social ambiguity is, I realize, not complete, but it is sufficient as a theoretical framework for the discussion of modern man's position in an increasingly abstract society. The homo duplex theorem is to be seen as an anthropological model with the help of which we will analyze and interpret some of the main trends in modern society in general and in the past decade in particular.

Three categories in this anthropological model need further clarification, since they will play an important role in our further discussion: *meaning, reality* and *freedom*, seen by me as the fundamental and intrinsically related coordinates of human existence. The remainder of this chapter will be devoted to a discussion of these three categories. It can be skipped by those readers who are interested only in the main development of my argument.

Action and thought, connected by language, are the two poles in between which human life is extended.

Among the animals only man is able to reflect upon himself, his environment, his relationship with others. He is able to stop his activity in everyday life's routine in order to ask questions about this very activity and the various aspects of life. Some of these aspects concern the meaning of life, the reality of the surrounding world, the reliability of his sense observations and of his logical deductions, and, most important of all, the possibility of freedom. Man working upon nature constructs together with others in an ongoing activity and exchange of thoughts and experiences a "second nature" (society and culture) which provides him with stability, certainty, reassuring taken-for-grantedness, in short: shelter. Within the structures of this socio-cultural environment, man is simultaneously an acting, a thinking, and a speaking being.

Man has given many different and sometimes weird answers to the questions he raises. Philosophy and religion were for a long time the exclusive fields in which these questions and answers were formulated, and they were mostly of a mythological and metaphysical nature. Modern man, using the tools of scientific research, strives for answers in the frame of reference of various disciplines, called collectively the humanities and the social sciences. Psychology, sociology, history, linguistics, law, deal with the different aspects of man and human life, each of them applying in its own specific way the objective methods of science. Moreover, each of these disciplines formulates its specific problems in view of its specific scientific interests and within the methodological parameters of its specific field. Therefore the problems, the methods and the eventual answers are conditioned by the parameters of a specific field. Sociology cannot ask every question about human behavior; it formulates its specifically sociological problems within its own sphere of scientific interest as laid down in its methodological definitions of the field. The same can be said of all the other disciplines.

As a result, the various scientific approaches to man and human life have fragmented the "total man" of everyday experience into as many pieces as there are disciplines. The "man" of the humanities and social sciences is a fragmented creature of a necessarily artificial nature: he is homo sociologicus, homo psychologicus, homo economicus, a man who speaks (linguistics), who creates music (musicology) and literature, and who stands in a chain of events and generations (history). This same man can be reduced in a natural scientific way: he is a living organism with a body (physiology) whose health is continuously threatened (medicine). Perhaps there is still one discipline left that studies man fairly comprehensively, namely *anthropology*. As physical anthropology, it belongs to the natural sciences dealing with man's body and its evolution; as cultural anthropology it focuses on his socio-cultural and symbolic life in all its manifestations. It is a scientific discipline that studies man in a holistic way.

Recently philosophy, being naturally inclined to approach reality in a more general way, has been very strongly attracted by modern anthropology. As a matter of fact, philosophical reflections and speculations about man have received a fresh and stimulating impetus from this relatively young discipline. In Europe the outcome of this has been given the somewhat irksome name of *philosophical anthropology*.

Philosophical anthropology is neither a specific discipline within philosophy, like epistemology or ontology, nor a particular philosophical school, like existentialism or analytic philosophy. It lies somewhere between philosophy and the sciences. Being too strongly rooted in biology, zoology, physiology and the social sciences to be called "philosophy" (if we conceive the latter as a metaphysical and deductive mode of thinking), it transcends the strict parameters of empirical science in order to arrive at ontological statements as to the nature of man and his sociocultural environment. Actually, this current of thought may be viewed as a historical necessity in the present development of Europe. The different philosophical schools in Europe wound up in a deadlock after German idealism collapsed under the stress of empiricism; after Marxism and existentialism became fixed ideologies; and after analytic philosophy had dried up in formalistic "logicisms." Meanwhile, a sound analysis of man's position in the modern world appeared to be more imperative than ever before. The bewildering events of two world wars and the awareness of impending political and social dangers demanded a more relevant philosophy than the former "isms" were able to present. Philosophers began to listen to the humanities and social sciences, scientists started to think in philosophical frames of reference. Analyses and interpretations of man's position in nature and society, of his essential traits and abilities, and of his position in modern society with its chances and dangers, all converged in what might be called philosophical anthropology, an interdisciplinary attempt to understand and interpret man.

Philosophical anthropology can, of course, be found from Plato and Aristotle to Kant, Hegel and Heidegger. What is new here is its foundation in the empirical sciences. Men like Koehler, Lorenz, Portmann, Gehlen, Buytendijk, and Plessner devoted themselves (often quite isolated from the established philosophical schools and their mutual quarrels) to a scientific-philosophical account of man and his world. A very heterogeneous group of scholars, some of them biologically (zoologically) oriented, like Portmann and Lorenz, others more influenced by traditional philosophy, like Gehlen, others applying the phenomenological approach, like Plessner and Buytendijk, still others under the spell of Marxism or existentialism, shared the common desire to open a debate on man's position in his world.[34]

One of the essential insights gained from philosophical anthropology is the fact that <u>man bestows meaning upon his environment</u>. The natural and socio-cultural world around us bears the signatures of our humanity. The other whom I encounter is not just a body, i.e. a physical object, ready for objective research; he is to me a person loaded with human meaning. Of course, we often reduce the other to an object, reifying him into a manipulated thing (as Marx observed in capitalist society). But this alienation shows once more how fundamental the category meaning is.

One can illustrate this by a simple example. In one of his latest publications, the Dutch psychologist Buytendijk tries to outline a philosophico-anthropological (mainly phenomenological) physiology.[35] His basic problem is the relationship between the natural-scientific knowledge of *a body* and the experience of *my body*. Physiology as an empirical science speaks about a neutral and objective thing—the body we have. But the physiologist may never forget that human beings not only *have* a body but also and primarily *are* a body and experience it in a subjective way. In other words, the physiologist has to take into account that man constitutes a psychosomatic unity.

Mead made a similar observation in his distinction of body and self. The body can be there and operate without any involvement on the part of the self. But the subjective experiences of the body are organized about a self: "The foot and hand belong to the self. We can see our feet, especially if we look at them from the wrong end of an opera glass, as strange things which we have difficulty in recognizing as our own."[36] By such a manipulation, in other words, we alienate our body into a strange object. In normal circumstances, however, we experience the body and its parts as extension pieces of our self. The same holds true, according to Mead, for the relation to our physical environment: it is organized about our self. For example: I walk through the room, pass chairs and a table, open a drawer and take a piece of paper in order to write a letter. This room is *my* room organized around *me* in reference to *my* activities. That means, this room responds to me by stimulating my activity. This chair "invites" me to sit down and the bed tempts me to lie on it. The objects constitute a "physical me" and I merge with them. It is quite amazing to find in Mead such a clear description of the phenomenological categories of meaning and intentionality.

Although he may definitely not be called a phenomenologist, it was Max Weber who in the field of sociology opened the gates for a phenomenologically oriented theory. His methodological rule to focus sociologically on subjectively intended meaning (*subjektiv gemeinter Sinn*) was rooted in the phenomenological awareness that social reality consists of subjectively experienced meaning rather than objectively existing systems and structures. One must always keep in mind the anti-metaphysical nature of Weber's concept *Sinn*. It does not signify any independent "objective" meaning inherent to social structures (such as the "meaning of the State" in Hegelian terms). Weber's concept refers rather to the subjective meaning people experience in their actions.

Meaning then is that aspect of social actions that distinguishes them from mere causal (physical or chemical) processes. The mixing and blending of chemicals is a "blind" event, intrinsically different from a football game in which people act according to established roles and pre-defined rules for the sake of a specific aim. The chemical blending does not possess any subjective meaning; the football game on the other hand is a complex whole of actions and interactions driven by subjective intentions. As a totality or configuration the football game has a general meaning (embodied in rules and regulations), understandable to insiders only. Not acquainted with this general meaning, the outsider will merely perceive a strange mixture of gestures and actions without any "logic." Indeed, each gesture and act receives its specific meaning from the general meaning, which is a traditionally inherited one.

This general meaning of the game is not only embodied by the rules and regulations but also expressed by the aim all the players have in mind when playing the game. Their particular intentions are directed by this aim, which thus molds their actions into a rational, aim-oriented behavior. Only in this way do the actions and interactions on the field become meaningful and understandable. For the outsider, these players perform most unusual movements and gestures, to many insiders they are the heroes of an almost solemn event. If they perform acts not understandable to these insiders, i.e. if they do not comply with the rules and regulations of the game, they will encounter sanctions of various sorts. Specific functionaries have been instituted to safeguard individual compliance with the general meaning of the game. Hence, subjective meaning is understandable only if it conforms to the intersubjectively accepted general meaning expressed in the aim of the game. In sum, a football game may be seen as a *meaningful configuration* which encompasses all individual acts and makes them understandable. This, of course, holds true of all institutions.

If we keep in mind that society is merely a compilation of such meaningful configurations, the concept of subjective meaning cannot be confused with a one-sided psychological reality. The subjective meaning is the intention of an act, goal-oriented toward a meaningful configuration and conditioned by it. A society enters, therefore, into a crisis if its members are, for whatever reason, no longer able to experience intersubjective meanings. In such a situation, complaints about anomie and alienation will multiply and a search for new meanings becomes the prime preoccupation of those who feel estranged and alienated.

Along with meaning and freedom, the concept of reality is the other basic category in our discussion. As in the case of meaning, one can speak easily about reality in metaphysical terms. As a matter of fact, too often the concept "social reality" acquires a metaphysical momentum in social theory. A concept that denotes merely the regular behavior of people within the structure of a meaningful configuration, called "society," is hypostasized into an ontological thing. In terms of our example, it is a legitimate question to ask what else a football game actually is than a name for a totality of meaningful actions. It draws its reality only from the fact that people assign a certain meaning to certain actions and decide to act accordingly. People, one might say, design collectively a meaningful configuration ("football game") which acquires its reality from the fact that men ("football players") perform certain intentional actions according to established rules and regulations. Sanctions are formulated to maintain and strengthen the reality of this designed configuration.

One can easily understand that the concepts meaning and reality cannot be sharply differentiated. They are to be viewed as correlates within one phenomenon. The following distinction may then be introduced: meaning is the quality of social behavior that makes it understandable and more or less predictable. This quality has a subjective and objective pole. Meaning is subjective in so far as each individual acts in accordance with certain intentions and goal-orientations. It is objective because it transcends individual behavior as intersubjectively accepted and traditional meaning (i.e. as meaning configuration or institution). Both aspects of meaning are dialectically related: the behavior of individual football players has subjective meaning because each individual player acts in accordance with an established meaning configuration, called football game. Reality is *the fact that* people act meaningfully and that their actions are subjectively and objectively understandable. This means that an individual role player loses his sense of reality if he no longer can predict and understand the behavior of others, and if he is no longer able to act according to the expectations others have of him as role player.

At this point, W. I. Thomas' famous theorem "If men define situations as real, they are real in their consequences," becomes pertinent. Social reality consists of situations in which human beings act and interact meaningfully. So long as these situations are experienced as meaningful and defined as real, they will be meaningful and real in their consequences, since the very actions realize the definition. The definition is the symbolic expression of the meaning of a situation and people will orient their actions toward it.

Thomas' theorem is helpful in avoiding hypostatization of

the concept "social reality." Weber's methodology offers still another device against this kind of logical aberration. Whereas many sociologists, particularly in American structural functionalism and the structuralist school of British anthropology, speak about institutions and social structures in terms of substantive entities, Weber always stressed the use of probabilistic categories. Defined in a Weberian way, an institution is *the chance that* predictable meaningful behavior will take place. Being continually aware of the dangers of conceptual reification, Weber defined all of social reality in terms of possibilities and chances. Power, to take another example, is not defined by Weber as a substantive reality innate in societal structures, but as the chance someone has to realize his own will over against the will of others. If this chance is great one possesses much power; if this chance is nil one happens to be powerless. Incidentally, it is in this sense that one must interpret Weber's rather abundant use of quotation marks in matters of social realities: they are "real" only in so far as they have the chance to be realized in behavior.

If we combine Thomas' theorem with Weber's nominalism, we get some interesting theoretical results. Human actions are not predictable and understandable because social structures and institutions possess any independent "objective" reality that conditions behavior through social control; human beings define situations as real and "create" reality by acting according to these definitions. If we know how men and women manage to live together in dyadic relationships that are defined as real, we may legitimately speak of an institution, called "marriage," as the chance that a particular (i.e. understandable and predictable) behavior will occur. We might then focus on the aspect of predictability itself: we can observe social roles that embody the definitions of the situation in a sedimentary way, existing to a certain degree independently of living individuals, namely before they were born and after they have died. Only then might we speak about an objective social reality.

Sociology can focus on the established predictable ways of behavior, i.e. on social roles. These roles are formalistic realities in that they constitute *ways of acting*. And a sociologist may limit his analyses to these forms of behavior. Georg Simmel's "formalistic sociology" is a good example. Émile Durkheim's stress on the social facts of "collective representations" and all forms of structural functionalism are two other examples. A more phenomenologically oriented sociology, however, will direct its attention primarily to the reality-producing and reality-maintaining processes.

So far we have defined meaning as a subjectively intentional or objectively institutional quality of human behavior, and reality as a process of realization in the sense of defining situations as being real and acting accordingly. We must now focus on a third category of social life that is closely related to meaning and reality, namely the concept of freedom.

Sociologists are generally inclined to leave the problem of freedom to philosophers, and if they venture any statements about it they are liable to derail rather catastrophically. There are logical reasons for this. It is impossible to speak about freedom in scientific, i.e. causal and value-free, terms because freedom belongs to a logically different frame of reference. Peter L. Berger has explained this in a lucid and simple manner by comparing the concepts of causality and freedom to those of utility and beauty.[37] We can empirically show the utility of human artifacts. It can be proved that a chair is an "instrument" to sit on. But one cannot demonstrate the beauty of this chair because the statement "This chair is nice" depends on a normative scale of values rooted in the subjective realm of taste. A similar relationship occurs between causality and freedom. One can empirically show the causality of a social action, but one can never prove that this action originated in human freedom. Or, to quote Alfred Schuetz, sociological theory is built up of analytic models which were constructed by the social scientist. The model is ruled exclusively by causality, and the people that inhabit the model are not real people with individual biographies and private life experiences, but puppets, *homunculi*, created by the social scientist and obeying his demands. If these puppets are free in their actions, they are so because the social scientist bestowed this freedom on them for the sake of his experiments.[38]

It is, however, precisely these analytic models that give us the opportunity to observe the kind and degree of freedom human beings actually enjoy in everyday life. Compared to these deterministic models, man in everyday life appears to be free to a considerable degree. A similar point was made by Max Weber when he spoke about the difficult methodological problem of the causal understanding of irrational behavior. Irrational motivations leading to irrational actions (e.g. a person's rage that leads him to irrational destructive acts) can be understood scientifically, according to Weber, only if this understanding occurs on a rational and causal level. An ideal type (i.e. a rational model based on causality) is constructed, and *by comparing* this rational model with the irrational motivations and actions, we will be able to see the irrationality of the act and to understand it rationally as well as causally. In the same way, by comparing the causal model and its puppets with real life, the social scientist is able to "discover" how much man in everyday life is a puppet indeed and to what extent he appears to be a free man with his own will and creativity.

There is still another way to discuss the problem of freedom within a scientific frame of reference.[39] One can put aside the question of the ontological reality of freedom and assume it a priori. Let us assume that man has freedom irrespective of its nature and possibilities. The valid question then is how man experiences this freedom in everyday life. We are now speaking about freedom in the same way we did about meaning and reality. Whether there is objective meaning to social reality and whether society is, objectively speaking, "real," are philosophical and theological questions that can be discussed only on a normative-ontological level. Subjectively experienced meaning and the continuous construction of reality, however, are processes that can be investigated empirically. The same holds true for freedom as the experience and awareness that man is more than a puppet, that he is able to realize his life and to provide it with meaning. Defined in this way, freedom is activity based on the awareness that man is more than a *homunculus*. It is essentially the construction of meaningful reality itself.

Meaning, reality and freedom thus intrinsically belong together. Our analytic thinking is inclined to separate them, but in everyday life they are intertwined as the three basic co-ordinates of human life. Freedom is the awareness that man is not passively enduring life, as if he were the victim of overwhelming metaphysical forces; the awareness that man can realize life in a meaningful way, despite the fact that human life is conditioned by natural and social limitations; the awareness that man can work within and upon these very limitations, that he can eventually change them for his own benefit. Therefore, technological and social evolution can be interpreted in the light of human freedom, i.e. of man's continuous attempt to transcend limits and boundaries, to say "no" to existing circumstances. Freedom is, finally, not just awareness—it is the realization and production of meaning itself. It is activity, or, to use Karl Marx's term, *praxis*.

In his *Theses on Feuerbach* (1845), Marx argues against Feuerbach's vulgar materialism. As much as he admired Feuerbach for his critique of Hegelian idealism, he rejected his notion of a sensual reality exterior to man and experienced by him in an aesthetic way. Feuerbach got caught in a strange dualism: on the one hand, he observed inert objective reality; on the other hand, he saw human beings passively experiencing this reality. To Marx, man is not a passively enduring being, but an explorer and creator. Not aesthetic experience but praxis is man's essential feature. Man is not victim of an inert reality, but the continuous producer of reality. This produced reality may acquire a momentum of its own and alienate man's freedom, but that is a historical and not a metaphysical process: in revolution man can do away with alienating structures and create a genuine "realm of freedom."

In the *Theses on Feuerbach*, Marx formulated the fundamental theme of philosophical anthropology: man is an acting being, he is a reality-creating, externalizing animal. This action is his freedom and provides him with the experience of meaning.

We will see in a later stage of our argument how modern man in our age of consumption seems to realize Feuerbach's "false" anthropology by reducing himself to a subjectivistic and aesthetic-emotional consumer who floats on short-term opinions, sudden emotions and short-range fashions, manipulated by the forces of an abstract society and remote from the essential human characteristic that Marx called praxis. Modern man defines institutions as alienating things and searches for absolute meaning, absolute freedom and utter reality in the emotional abodes of his subjectivity.

Unlike the animal, man has to construct a surrounding world of institutions. Within their parameters, he has to realize his freedom and to experience his meanings. Man cannot afford to remain isolated in his search for meaning, reality and freedom, driven by what Marx has called modern man's "Robinson Crusoe ideology." Neither can he afford to search for meaning, reality and freedom in the emotional and unsteady abodes of his subjectivity. Praxis is man's condition, and his existence can evolve only through exteriority, i.e. through estrangement by a non-subjective, outer reality which functions as his field of expression and shields him from the terrors of blind emotionalism.

It is at this point that we must realize that the technological-industrial complex called "modern society" has brought man to a very hazardous situation. This society, as we will see, has developed gradually into an abstract and highly segmented superstructure which increasingly seems to live its own life, conditioning man in all the fibers of his existence and reducing him more and more to a one-sided *homo externus*. It is only against the background of this abstract society that one can understand and assess modern man's behavior, particularly the behavior of those who have to live in this society for the coming five or six decades. The following chapters are devoted to a discussion of this very complex group of problems.

NOTES

1. See for a discussion of subjective and objective time: A. C. Moulyn, *Structure, Function and Purpose* (New York: The Liberal Arts Press, 1957).
2. A historical survey of this problem in traditional philosophy is presented by G. W. Hylkema, *Homo Duplex* (Haarlem: De Erven Bohn, NV, 1963).
3. "Denn ich sonst offt gesagt habe, das man die zwey unter-

scheiden muss, Ampt und Person. Es ist viel ein ander man, der
der Hans oder Martin heisset und der Kurfurst odder Doctor
und prediger heisst." Quoted from F. Lau, *Luthers Lehre von
den beiden Reichen* (Berlin: Luthertum Heft 8, 1953), p. 30.

4. "Also hat ein iglich mensch auff erden zwo person: Eine fuer
sich selbst, an niemand verbunden denn an Gott alleine,
darnach eine weltliche damit er an ander Leut gebunden ist."
Quoted from Harald Diem, *Luthers Lehre von den zwei
Reichen* (Muenchen, 1938), p. 28.

5. Cf. Karl Loewith, *Das Individuum in der Rolle des Mit-
menschen,* 1928 (Darmstadt: Wissenschaftliche Buchgesellschaft, 1962), pp. 8–11.

6. W. I. Thomas, *On Social Organization and Social Personality,*
ed. M. Janowitz (Chicago: Phoenix Books, 1966), p. 23.

7. *Ibid.,* p. 13.

8. *Ibid.,* p. 35.

9. *Ibid.,* p. 32.

10. *Ibid.,* p. 259.

11. *Ibid.,* pp. 258 f.

12. *Ibid.,* p. 26.

13. *Ibid.,* p. 27.

14. *Ibid.,* pp. 27 f.

15. *Ibid.,* p. 28.

16. *Ibid.,* p. 29.

17. G. H. Mead, *Mind, Self and Society,* 1934, ed. C. W. Morris
(Chicago: University of Chicago Press, 1959), p. 15.

18. *Ibid.,* p. 18.

19. See for this example, *ibid.,* p. 109.

20. *Ibid.,* p. 175.

21. *Ibid.,* p. 262.

22. *Ibid.,* p. 174.

23. Idem.

24. *Ibid.,* pp. 273 ff.

25. Émile Durkheim, *The Elementary Forms of Religious Life,*
1912, transl. by J. Swain (New York: Collier Books, 1961),
p. 29.

26. I elaborated this theme in greater detail in a Dutch publication
with the title "Het Sociale Dilemma en Karl Marx," Eltheto
Brochure Reeks Nr. 21, July 1966.

27. Georg Simmel, "How is Society Possible?" in G. Simmel et al.,
Essays on Sociology, Philosophy and Aesthetics, ed. K. H.
Wolff (New York: Harper Torchbooks, 1965), p. 347.

28. *Ibid.,* pp. 347 f.

29. *Ibid.,* p. 350.

30. Ralf Dahrendorf, "Homo Sociologicus," in *Essays in the Theory
of Society* (Stanford, Cal.: Stanford University Press, 1968),
pp. 19–88.

31. Dahrendorf discussed these criticisms in an essay called "Sociology and Human Nature," *ibid.*, pp. 88–107.

32. Helmuth Plessner, "Soziale Rolle und Menschliche Natur," in *Erkenntnis und Verantwortung*, Festschrift fuer Theodor Litt (Duesseldorf, 1960), pp. 105–16. Cf. by the same author, *Das Problem der Oeffentlichkeit und die Idee der Entfremdung*, Goettinger Universitaetsreden, 28 (Goettingen, 1960).

33. Cf. Arnold Gehlen, *Studien zur Anthropologie und Soziologie* (Neuwied-Berlin: Luchterhand Verlag, 1963) and his *Der Mensch. Seine Natur und Seine Stellung in der Welt*, 1940 (Frankfurt a.M.-Bonn: Athenaeum Verlag, 1962). See also Peter L. Berger, Hansfried Kellner, "Arnold Gehlen and the Theory of Institutions," *Social Research* 32:1 (1965) 110 ff., and my Dutch dissertation *Institutionalisering* (Hilversum: Paul Brand, 1967), chapter 4, pp. 105–28.

34. See next to Gehlen the following literature: Jakob von Uexkuell, *Streifzuege durch die Umwelten von Tieren und Menschen* (Hamburg: Rowohlt Verlag, 1956), F. J. J. Buytendijk, *Mensch und Tier* (Muenchen: Rowohlt Verlag, 1961), A. Portmann, *Zoologie und das Neue Bild des Menschen* (Muenchen: Rowohlt Verlag, 1960), Konrad Lorenz, *Ueber Tierisches und Menschliches Verhalten* Gesammelte Abhandlungen I und II (Muenchen: Piper Verlag, 1966) and K. Lorenz, *Das Sogenannte Boese* (Wien: Borotha-Schoeler Verlag, 1963) transl. as *On Aggression* by M. K. Wilson (New York: Harcourt, 1966) and M. Latzke (London: Methuen, 1966). A "classic" in the field of philosophical anthropology is Max Scheler, *Die Stellung des Menschen im Kosmos* (*Man's Place in Nature*).

35. F. J. J. Buytendijk, *Prolegomena van een anthropologische Fysiologie* (Utrecht-Antwerpen: Aula, 1965).

36. G. H. Mead, *o.c.*, p. 136.

37. Peter L. Berger, *Invitation to Sociology* (New York: Doubleday Anchor, 1963), p. 124.

38. Alfred Schutz, *Collected Papers*, Vol. I (The Hague: Nijhoff, 1962), p. 41.

39. Peter L. Berger, *o.c.*, p. 142.

3

ABSTRACT SOCIETY

Introduction

In the previous chapter we constructed the theoretical stage
on which our successive arguments about man in industrial
society will be developed. A theoretical picture was given of
man in his socio-cultural world: a double being, social and
individual, conditioned and free; a being who needs surrounding social structures in order to be human, to experience
meaning, reality and freedom.

It is now time to ask more precisely what man's position is
in modern industrial and bureaucratic society. How do things
look when we apply the homo duplex theorem to contemporary society?

There are two main problems. Seen in the light of the
homo duplex theorem, we must determine first what the nature of contemporary society is and how it affects modern
man and his consciousness. This requires a historical and
comparative analysis of industrial society. The present chapter will be devoted to this task. But we must determine, in
the second place, how modern man reacts to this society, how
he copes with the problems of social control and alleged
alienation. This will be taken up in the next chapter on "the
spirit of protest."

I will begin with a somewhat loaded and perhaps presumptuous statement, which I hope will gain more subtle
dimensions during the course of the argument. Modern society
is an essentially abstract society which is increasingly unable
to provide man with a clear awareness of his identity and a
concrete experience of meaning, reality and freedom. This
abstract nature of society is caused primarily by its *pluralism,* i.e. by its segmentation of its institutional structure.
Compared to tribal societies and their overarching kinship

systems, or to medieval society with its rather uniform, namely Christian, structure of meaning, modern society appears to be chaotically pluralistic. As a result of this pluralism society has lost, as we will see in greater detail later, much of its existential concreteness. The abstract nature of modern society is sufficiently illustrated by such modern cultural expressions as abstract painting and sculpture and electronic music. On the level of interpersonal relationships the abstract nature of contemporary society is illustrated by the fact that a large number of the personal face-to-face relations of premodern society have been replaced by the relations of official functionaries who practice the roles of their social positions.

It is, however, rather meaningless to assert that modern society grew abstract, since in a way each society is abstract by its very nature. "Society," we must realize, is nothing but a concept which refers to the actions and interactions of countless individuals. As such, it shares with all other concepts the quality of being general and abstract. It needs some of Max Weber's nominalism to avoid any conceptual reification on this point. Moreover, one must bear in mind that those structured actions and interactions called "society" are themselves formalistic and thus abstract. "Society" is the name we give to specific forms of behavior and *as forms* they are naturally abstract. It was mainly Georg Simmel's "formalistic sociology" that made this point clear.

Therefore, by saying that in the process of modernization society became increasingly abstract, I obviously mean to say that *modern society has become abstract in the experience and consciousness of man!* Modern man, that is, does not "live society," he faces it as an often strange phenomenon. This society has lost more and more of its reality and meaning and seems to be hardly able to function as the holder of human freedom. As a result, many modern men are turning away from the institutions of society and searching for meaning, reality and freedom elsewhere. These three co-ordinates of human existence have become the scarce values of a continuous existential demand.

I define the concept "abstract society" as follows: modern society is, in the experience and consciousness of man, very concrete as to its coercive forces of control, but it evaporates into an awareness of loss of meaning, reality and freedom when modern man tries to keep this coercion under control and to evade the sense of absurdity and inauthenticity.

This definition will be elaborated in the next pages. But we must first look further into the phenomenon of abstraction itself.

The Nature of Abstraction

I shall restrict myself to only those aspects of abstraction that bear upon the main points of my argument. There is, to begin with, the epistemological fact that man is able by means of thought and language to generalize particular pieces of reality into abstract concepts. The capacity to generalize is the source of all of our communication: if I use the word "tree" in one of my sentences, everyone will perform the act of generalization with me and, apart from specific situations, remain on the level of this generalization, without asking me such questions as "Which tree? Of which shape and color? Where?" Almost all of our linguistic intercourse occurs on such a level of abstraction. But we particularize quite a lot too. If I tell somebody about my experiences of the phenomenon "father," I have to come down to a certain level of concreteness by using the concept "my father" and by summing up some of the main characteristics of this particular father. There is hardly any other way to explain what I mean when I speak about my experiences of the phenomenon "father"—unless I am a poet transforming these experiences to the new reality of a poem.

Without entering the traditional philosophical debates on "realism" and "nominalism," we may conclude that human communication occurs in an ongoing movement between generalizations and particularizations, between abstraction and specification. But what is more important, if the experience of an abstract phenomenon (e.g. "father") cannot be brought down to an experience of a particular phenomenon (e.g. "my father"), meaning and reality will vanish. In such a case, we are in danger of speaking and experiencing non-sense.

As the last example indicates, abstraction may easily lead

to serious mistakes in our thinking and conceiving. These logical faults, in their turn, can have fateful social consequences, as Karl Marx indicated by his concept "false consciousness." In terms of our discussion, *false consciousness* presents a logical manipulation whereby abstract phenomena are treated as if they were real and concrete. Taking the example up once more, to speak in the course of everyday life about the general phenomenon "father" as if it were a real entity, without ever particularizing it to "my father" is an act of false consciousness. A perfect example is the Freudian mythology of the Father-figure supposedly towering high above all of us, not just as a concept but as a force which determines a substantial portion of our behavior and psychic life. As a matter of fact, this definition of the situation might have become real in its consequences: after several decades of Freudianism, the psychoanalytic Father has obtained so many real dimensions that almost none of us seems able to resist the Oedipus complex any more!

Marx applied the concept of "false consciousness," which incidentally he also called "reification" (i.e. making abstract concepts into real things), to social and economic circumstances in capitalist society. In the eyes of the capitalist, everything and everyone (and especially the worker with his productive working power) is conceived of in terms of commodities that can be bought and sold. The capitalist is totally entangled in the "fetishism of commodities" and the veneration of abstract realities. He is particularly possessed by the abstraction par excellence: money. Abstract things, not human beings, rule over capitalist society. Man in this society, worker as well as capitalist, exploited and exploiter, are alienated from their true nature.

The gist of Marx's argument can be applied to a much broader frame of reference. Joseph Gabel, for instance, in his study *La Fausse Conscience* (1962) argues that the reification of abstract phenomena can be interpreted in psychiatric terms as schizophrenia, that is, as a kind of logical disease in which man constructs an abstract world but treats it as if it were real and concrete. Indeed, the reality of the schizophrenic is abstract and alienated from the realities of everyday life.[1] This explains why one experiences such a strong feeling of estrangement when communicating with schizo-phrenics: one encounters a seemingly real and rational world which, however, is abstract and phantomlike, and thus unreal and irrational.

Philosophical and religious metaphysics constitute still an-other field that is full of examples of abstract reifications. Reduced to its essence, metaphysics can be defined as a logi-cal manipulation whereby man constructs abstract realities (gods, spirits, soul, etc.) and then treats or even worships them as if they were real and concrete. One step further and these abstract realities are proclaimed to be the first, the original, the genuinely "real" realities from which all other natural and social reality emanates and receives its being: "The gods created the world," or: "The Spirit rules over his-tory and the human mind." Primitive religions, Platonism, Thomism and Hegelianism are as many examples of this logical manipulation whereby abstract projections become the archetypes for all reality.[2] Mythology, as Mircea Eliade shows time and again, is the proper locus of such reified archetypes.[3]

We must now focus on the more specifically social dimen-sions of abstraction. To begin with, the awareness of abstrac-tion increases with the increase of distance and size. Life in a small and rural community presents a good example. If this community is not affected yet by the emigration of younger generations to the urban and industrial centers, the villager will experience his society as a concrete reality. Social control, strong as it may be in this small Gemeinschaft-setting, can still be grasped as being necessary and meaningful. It is part and parcel of the taken-for-granted world. Since everybody knows his place in the local hierarchy of status, power and prestige, one has a clear experience and understanding of identity. In this concrete meaning structure, existential free-dom and authenticity are not problematic points of discussion but taken-for-granted realities. Their very unproblematic taken-for-grantedness is their concreteness!

However, social life in the pre-industrial Gemeinschaft-setting is not entirely concrete. Parts of this world are abstract because they are distant and remote from everyday reality. It is the social and/or geographic distance that makes them

abstract as "unreal"
not experienced

<u>abstract in the experience of man.</u> For example, if our community is located somewhere in rural Europe, the priest in his vicarage, representative of an overwhelmingly impressive and almost universal institution, might acquire some abstract characteristics. Even more so the count in his castle outside the village—an almost mythological figure around whom legends are woven. This sense of abstraction grows with the increase of social distance. High in the clouds of abstraction dwell the political leaders of the country: abstract figures, never seen by anybody in the village in a face-to-face relation. Their abstraction increases because of their geographic remoteness: these leaders rule in the capital, far away.

To rural and closed communities, the big city bears the image of a strange Babylon. Since it represents an abstract and empty reification, this image can be filled up with several, often contradictory legends. The metropolis, often referred to as the Big City, is the paradoxical place of both seductions and unlimited possibilities, of dangers and unheard-of chances. Today, we are urbanized to such a degree that we are hardly capable of understanding what this "Babylonian" image of the Big City means to the rural mind. It performs the same function as those strange and faraway countries in legends and fairy tales. After his homecoming, Ulysses can tell strange stories about remote and abstract people with strange customs and gruesome beliefs. But hearing these stories, one feels more at home in one's own world. After all, the estrangement from the taken-for-granted and meaningful world was just a tale.

This kind of abstract experience of socially and geographically distant phenomena is not, of course, restricted to pre-industrial communities of the Gemeinschaft type. To many Europeans whose knowledge of America stems largely from the products of Hollywood (next to Madison Avenue the biggest producer of abstract images), the word "America" contains all sorts of mythological connotations—"the land of unprecedented wealth and opportunities," or "the country of frightening superficiality." The moment these Europeans enter into the United States, either as immigrants or as visitors, they receive a severe shock: the abstract images and concrete reality clash. This is not to say that the image was altogether wrong. The best way to put it is as follows: the splendor Hollywood presents is far from real, the superficiality it reflects is less than dominant.

Social distance leads to similar kinds of abstraction. Even today, the famous "power elite" at the top of the socio-political and socio-economic ladder are not much more than the bearers of abstract images, professionally constructed by the so-called image builders. Leading politicians, for instance, occupy a place in our consciousness that is pretty much isolated from the concrete experiences of everyday existence. Actually, they are not much more than pictures on our television screens, circling around such legendary places as the Capitol or the White House. Even the familiarity with which medieval man could think about his monarch as a patrimonial ruler is no longer possible. We moderns have no existential notion of the power elite that rules over us. It dwells in executive offices, preferably located in the top floor of steel-and-glass skyscrapers.

Naturally, the experience of abstraction increases with the increase of social distance. The White House is not just the home of a President, but a national symbol, or, in Hegelian terms, an Idea that represents the presidency, the government, the whole nation. It is an abstraction with metaphysical and mythological qualities. Note the anthropomorphic way in which this mansion is usually mentioned. It can think and speak like a human being, as in newspaper sentences such as "No comment could be obtained from the White House," or "The White House released the following statement." Another dimension of this particular abstraction is that the man who occupies the White House appears as a kind of super-abstraction. He is not so much this particular man with this particular biography (these aspects are usually covered by the various ladies' journals as mere gossip material), as the President, holder of an abstract position with almost unconceivable power—the player of a most conspicuous and most anonymous role. This abstraction has traditionally been expressed by the custom of referring to several of these men by their initials instead of their full names. Man's unique identity is covered by his name, whereas initials are able to wrap up this identity in anonymity and abstraction. The President, that is, FDR, JFK, or LBJ.

Abstraction, I said before, also increases with size. If a rural community modernizes and grows into a big industrial metropolis, it will become abstract. Face-to-face relationships will shrink into a few friendships based on the individualistic principles of privacy and difficult to maintain because of social and geographic mobility. For the rest, they will be replaced by anonymous roles imposed on man by a rationally organized society in which efficiency rates higher than the human dimensions of life. Moreover, the well established equilibrium of producer and consumer in the personality structure of pre-modern man is gradually replaced in the process of modernization by a broken relationship within the modern individual between the functionary and player of roles on the one hand and the consumer of countless commodities offered in a dazzling supply on the mass market, on the other.

Marx, as we saw before, was one of the first to point out the alienation resulting from the domination of man by abstract forces. False consciousness, which reduces man to a thing and commodity and thereby perverts his freedom in a state of slavery, is a mode of existence that is entirely entangled in an abstract world, remote from everyday reality and meaning. It is a state of estrangement that leaves man under the spell of abstract forces.

Today Marx's alienation theory has gained a dubious popularity and serves as a key denominator for existentialist dissatisfactions. Therefore, it must be stressed at this point that man needs the alienation of abstraction (i.e. the negation of his reality) to a certain degree. He needs it in order to feel at home again in his traditional, taken-for-granted world. Legends and mythologies about strange people in remote countries or about mythological figures in pre-historic days function as mirrors that enable man to believe more firmly and understand more clearly his everyday reality and taken-forgranted meaning structures. They are a looking glass that offers a magnificent opportunity to wander around in aweinspiring strange worlds. Such odysseys through abstraction make homecoming desirable and the burdens of everyday life more bearable. They are techniques of confirming meaning and reality. <u>Alienation, however, becomes unbearable and socially dysfunctional</u> *if there is no homecoming any more*, if everyday life itself becomes abstract and strange, losing its meaning and reality; if legends and myths replace reality and experience. In such a case, man is no longer facing abstraction but experiencing it in every fiber of his existence. Life itself has become a myth.

The Nature of Abstract Society

The following section is not a historical account of the birth and development of modern society. Such an account would require a comprehensive discussion of the historical phenomenon usually called modernization and obviously lies outside the limits of the present discussion. I shall restrict myself to a survey of the main characteristics of industrial society, which I have called an abstract society. This will consist of an idealtypical comparison of contemporary Western society and its predecessors, ancient Graeco-Roman and medieval society. In addition to this diachronic comparison, I will also compare, again in an idealtypical manner, our industrial society with non-industrial, developing societies.

It must be emphasized that such an approach in no way pretends to replace a precise historical account of facts and events. Through its generalizations, the idealtypical approach tries rather to demonstrate what the *typical characteristics* are of a particular historical phenomenon. A precise historical account of the process of modernization, indispensable as it is for a correct understanding of modern society, is not capable of projecting sharply and distinctively the characteristics of a historical phenomenon in a holistic way. In other words, digging in the ground on one spot is necessary, but a bird's eye view of the whole area of which this single spot is one constitutive part, opens dimensions and characteristics that could not be seen before. Or, in phenomenological terms, the generalizing idealtypical approach lays bare dimensions of meaning that characterize certain historical phenomena but are hardly seen by detailed empirical and historiographic research. The following pages are to be read with these comments in mind.

The birth of modern society was a sequence of several social, economic, political, religious, scientific, and technological revolutions. *Revolution,* one might say, is the main stigma of modern Western civilization, leaving heavy traces in the structure of society and the psychological constitution of man.

It is up to the historian to describe and analyze the revolutions that repeatedly shocked and reshaped Western civilization during the last four centuries. It is up to the sociologist to demonstrate how these revolutions kept the social systems of this civilization in an ongoing turmoil, changing the structures and meaning of their institutions often beyond the comprehension of the individuals living in them. It is up to the philosopher and the theologian to interpret these revolutions, which blew as so many thunderstorms through traditional beliefs and world views. The social psychologist, however, will try to examine the impact of revolutions on human consciousness, with, of course the help of the historian, the sociologist, the philosopher and the theologian. Revolution, he will argue, left its marks on the consciousness of modern man: he is unable to experience an ultimate order in which each part obtains a stable position, in which truth and freedom are embedded in a taken-for-granted manner, and from which everything and everyone deductively acquires meaning and reality. Most important of all, this loss of an ultimate order has deprived man of the solid ground upon which his identity was founded. Whereas man in ancient Greek society (or for that matter in tribal society, or in the Middle Ages) experienced life as being embedded in a circularly conceived cosmos where stability ruled and every change was seen as a repetition of what formerly had been, modern man seems to stay in an open universe with its co-ordinates crumbling off. He often seems to be left alone with a deep feeling of meaninglessness, unreality and absurdity. He knows a frightening awareness of being compelled to realize freedom and creativity without or even against traditional structures. These structures are experienced as empty fetters devoid of the meaning former generations put into them. Therefore, with revolution, a profound feeling of relativity and uncertainty has been engraved on the consciousness of post-medieval Western man. It often seems as if only the "road inward" is left as an escape from the pains of the situation. Next to *revolution* (the wish to run amok against traditional institutions) subjectivism (the flight from the frustrations of institutional existence) has put its stamp on the psychological constitution of man. One might call this a qualitative change of consciousness, as we will see later.

Antiquity and the Middle Ages reveal similar structures of social life and human consciousness. Medieval man, as well as the Greek or the Roman, experienced life as if it were rooted in an encompassing, more or less closed and stable cosmos. Romano Guardini formulated this very nicely: "Both see, and which is more important, experience the world as a confined structure, as a formed *Gestalt*—figuratively speaking as a ball."[4]

Man in this Ptolemaic cosmos is not seen as a being who realizes himself (his meaning, his reality and his freedom) in the floating process of an ever-changing history, but is rather looked at as a thinglike part of a stable world. He is not a unique individual with his particular mode of existence and subjectivity but rather a small particle in a huge, ordered, well-established universe.[5] His action is not an essential quality through which he poses himself in history but an accidental circumstance (an *accidens*) that can be explained only in terms of the cyclic and rational course of the cosmos. This man knows his place in the world. The functions and tasks of everyday life are not achieved by the individual but embody his ascribed social qualities. The social structures of this world are very little differentiated and thus still understandable. Today, such a comprehensiveness can be found only in relatively secluded areas of the world.

In addition to this, social life in antiquity was experienced as being ruled by the *Logos* as a rational principle that coordinates everything. Medieval man believed in a *God* who not only created this world and continues to sustain it but also rules over society, its institutions and its hierarchy. Greek *Logos* and medieval God were similar ruling principles of the world. Of course, these were abstract projections but—

and this is the crucial point—they were experienced in everyday life as concrete realities since they were believed to be embodied in the order of the *polis* and the hierarchy of the Church. Indeed, this world was a pre-established harmony —a perfect system in equilibrium.

The Greek knew he was taken care of by the concrete order of his *polis*—the relatively small city-state which was believed to be a micro-cosmos reflecting the order of the macro-cosmos. Obeying the rules of this polis, the Greek felt his freedom realized. Its structures were not viewed as alienating objective things. He related to his society as a part to an organic whole. In addition to this, he also felt related to the universe since he knew that his inner essence, the rationality and order of his being, emanated from that macro-cosmic essence called *Logos*. In short, feeling the shelter of his polis, the Greek experienced a firm bond between his own rational nature and the rationality of the universe. It is no wonder that control of passions and modesty were viewed as the fundamental virtues of Greek ethics. This philosophy of cosmic harmony and rational order had no place for passions of protest and revolt, because even the smallest disorder in the micro-cosmic might result in catastrophic disturbances of the macro-cosmic mechanism. The greatest danger was that man often disturbed this harmony without his knowledge or against his will, thus inflicting disasters upon himself and his fellow men. This was the problem of tragic guilt, dealt with by the tragedies of Aeschylus, Sophocles, and Euripides.[6]

This tragic fear, however, was kept in balance by a very fundamental feeling of certainty. Indeed, the Hellenes were very certain of their cause as is illustrated by their habit of calling their non-Greek neighbors "barbarians," which means "people who are not even able to speak Greek but utter sounds like bar-bar."[7]

In his famous *The Ancient City* (1864), N. D. Fustel de Coulanges warns against romanticizing the Greek polis as a perfect example of "direct democracy." He stresses the tyrannical aspects of the Greek city-state, which left the individual with very little freedom. It sounds almost like the description of a totalitarian society when he writes:

There was nothing independent in man; his body belonged to the state, and was devoted to its defense. At Rome military service was due till a man was fifty years old, at Athens till he was sixty, at Sparta always. His fortune was always at the disposal of the state. If the city had need of money, it could order the women to deliver up their jewels, the creditors to give up their claims, and the owners of olive trees to turn over gratuitously the oil which they had made.

Private life did not escape this omnipotence of the state. The Athenean law, in the name of religion, forbade man to remain single. Sparta punished not only those who remained single, but those who married late. . . . It was a common thing for the kind of dress to be invariably fixed by each city.[8]

This may be true, but the main question as to how the Greek experienced this absolutism was not discussed by Fustel de Coulanges. One should not romanticize the polis, as, for instance, Hegel did, seeing the Greek city-state as the perfect society. But one should also not impose our individualistic concept of freedom on this society. Man in this and similar pre-modern societies could not conceive of any individuality apart from a collectivity. To him, individual freedom was borne by the collectivity, which was seen as an organic totality that was always more than the isolated individual. To the Greek, individuality was safeguarded by the polis, which in turn was safeguarded by the harmony of the macro-cosmic universe.

Because of this cosmic world view, the Greeks were unable to develop any deeper awareness of history. The overarching cosmos had a cyclic and rational course in which every event was considered as a repetition of some previous event. In this "ball," to use Guardini's metaphor, everything turned on a central axis (the *Logos*) and thus followed a rational, predictable and fateful course. Life was not experienced as an open possibility to be realized by human initiative in an open world toward an open future, but as Fate conditioned by the "logic" of eternal return. Everything, even the time dimension, had its place in a cosmic circle where history appeared as nothing but eternal return. As the German theologian Rudolf

Bultmann has put it: "Historical events are understood in the same way as cosmic events; it is a movement in which through all changes the same thing happens in new constellations."[9] The historiography of Herodotus, Thucydides and Polybius was conditioned by this cosmic conception of life and history. They were concerned only with past events and exercised their historiography as some sort of natural science, not describing and interpreting events and processes but listing "things," frozen events of the past. Mircea Eliade's concept of the "neutralization of history," typical for all mythology, can be applied to Greek philosophy and historiography perfectly well.

With the decline of the polis after the Peloponnesian wars and the fall of Athens—events that shocked the taken-for-granted world of the Greeks beyond measure—*doubt* with regard to the rational order of the cosmos entered into the Greek mind. This doubt is particularly manifested by the cynicism and relativism of the Sophists—those Machiavellian interpreters of human existence—and found poetic expression in the tragedies of Euripides. Sophist individualism and Euripides' aesthetic subjectivism heralded the decay of the logical order of the Greeks. The harmonious cosmos crumbled in the experience and consciousness of its inhabitants, and it did so beyond repair. The succeeding Hellenistic empire, as we all know, was a mere outburst of power (especially after the Romans took over) and could never restore in the masses an awareness of security and meaning. The Hellenistic "cosmos" was an abstract universe in which man felt lonesome and estranged, and in which he longed for redemption. The time was ripe for religions and pseudo-religions of all sorts to blossom and flourish. They all offered man their particular redemption plan. Prominent among them were the Christian Church and a widespread, very vigorous sectarian movement called gnosticism. Coming from the East, gnosticism penetrated deep into the Hellenistic culture and nearly conquered the Christian Church, especially in its Manicheistic manifestation.

The gnostic religion preached the road that leads to the inner realms of man's subjectivity, where "deep down" his authenticity has remained captive in the chains of a material world. It promised its adherents the meaning, reality and freedom they had lost in the outer world of Hellenistic society by liberating them from the pains of *alienation* (a concept, incidentally, that originated in gnosticism). Man's fate in history, according to the gnostic religion, is the story of his fall from his spiritual and true origin into the chains of the material world where he is doomed to be alienated from his true self. But deep down in his soul, man still carries a spark of original light. By applying the secret knowledge (*gnosis*) of gnosticism, man can return to this origin and thus arrive at the spiritual truth of Life.

This kind of primeval depth-psychology never indicated much affinity toward the rationality and lucidity of the Greek *Logos*. Of course, gnosticism used the *Logos* concept but degraded it to a sultry mystery. Indeed, Greek rationality and lucidity were utterly alien to most gnostics. They preferred to embellish their systems of thought with the seemingly inscrutable wisdoms of the Orient. The slogan *Ex oriente lux* (Light comes from the East) was coined to indicate the kind of solution the gnostics had to offer. At any rate, syncretism as a mixture of countless religious ideas, tied together by the psychologistic tendencies of gnosticism and endowed with the mystic aromas of the Orient, succeeded the former certainty of the Greeks in their *polis*. Living in the big metropolitan centers of Alexandria, Constantinople and Rome, Hellenistic man drifted off to confusion, loneliness and alienation. Society, in short, was experienced as an abstract phenomenon. The situation was very similar to ours.

In such times of socio-cultural disintegration, single thinkers will usually arise who try to restore the old cosmos. These philosophers attempt to construct a system by which every aspect and element of life can be explained deductively. Such systems are theoretical devices for the neutralization of the cracks and ruptures in reality. They function as impressive ideologies that glue together *at an abstract level* what has been broken in the experience of *concrete everyday reality.* It was at the time of Sophist individualism and Euripides' subjectivism (fifth century B.C.) that Plato launched his cosmic philosophy of Ideas. As manifold, chaotic and pluralistic as reality may appear to be, it regains harmony and cohesiveness if it is interpreted Platonically as an emanation of metaphysical realities. In other words, Platonism is a masterful attempt to transfer all of reality to one cosmic, lofty, and abstract harmony—an attempt to be equaled in history only by Hegel. The latter, knowing perfectly well that his reconstruction of the cosmos consisted merely of projections of the mind, proclaimed this mind (*Geist*) as the primeval mover of history and the structuring principle of life. One may irreverently interpret these Platonic and Hegelian systems as delightful games of abstraction.

In medieval society, Platonism was certainly more than an abstract theory or a game of the mind. It really functioned (albeit in a theological travesty), because it happened to fit perfectly well in the constitution of the society. Platonism, adjusted to the demands of Christian theology, could explain and legitimate the structure of medieval society with its stratified hierarchy of the three estates. Having absorbed the Christian God as the highest Idea from which everything receives its being, Platonism served as a perfect conceptual model for medieval society. It was, of course, not able to explain all details of reality in a satisfactory manner, but for that purpose the Aristotelian system was used. Despite the profound differences between Aristotle and his teacher Plato, both their comprehensive systems rendered invaluable services in the Middle Ages. In brief, Aristotle provided the "empirical" interpretation and Plato the metaphysical legitimation of the medieval world.

According to applied Platonism, the heavenly hierarchy of archangels, angels and saints was represented on earth by the hierarchy of the estates, the latter being an emanation of the former. Thus the Pope in Rome as Christ's deputy on earth ruled with divine authority—a dignity soon appropriated by monarchs as well. In other words, abstract reality in heaven had its concrete counterpart on earth: *the macro-cosmos was in balance with the micro-cosmos again.* Various scholastic theological systems, particularly Thomas Aquinas' famous *Summa* must be viewed in this perspective. They present impressive bodies of knowledge that try to grasp all of medieval society (its economic, political, social and religious life) from one single point of view. Incidentally, these masterpieces of intellectual abstraction were composed with such devotion and such zeal that one suspects their authors foresaw with fear and trembling the approaching end of the medieval universe.

We may conclude that medieval man lived and thought under the spell of abstract metaphysics, but that this abstraction did not enter into his consciousness as an alienating force. On the contrary, social life was firmly rooted in a strict stratification pattern, which abstract metaphysics helped to explain and legitimate. In other words, medieval metaphysics strengthened the plausibility of the existing society. Therefore, theology and philosophy acquired a concrete and real momentum in the consciousness of medieval intellectuals (mainly the clergy) and a momentum of taken-for-granted truth in the consciousness of non-intellectuals (largely nobility, peasants and artisans).

However, these explanations and legitimations lost their monopoly and realistic contents when the structures of medieval society began to change. The powerful rise of the cities and their trading, would-be capitalist inhabitants; the Reformation joined by nationalist movements in northern Europe; the exploring expeditions opening new territories and different civilizations, were some of the main forces that brought the monolithic structure of medieval society to an end. Capitalism changed the economic and social structures. The Reformation destroyed the religious monopoly of the clergy and isolated the individual by placing all the emphasis on *his* faith and *his* responsibility. Nationalism attacked the political monopoly of the Vatican and increased political and social pluralisms. The discoveries of foreign regions and civilizations corroded the image of medieval society as the final and absolute norm of life.[10]

Of particular interest to this discussion is the rise of *nominalism* as a new philosophical school and a new form of consciousness. Having its roots in the twelfth century, nominalism reached its peak with William of Occam. In opposition to Platonically oriented realism, nominalism stressed the relevance of the empirical and the particular. Being essentially epistemological ("horse" is not an idea from which all particular horses draw their being but just a name for empirical animals with common features), nominalism deeply influenced medieval consciousness. The general, seen in the Platonic world view as source and origin of all being, was now proclaimed to be just a name for particular facts. Not the general but the particular is real. Imagine what this meant for the theological emanation doctrine, which saw God as the most general and thus most real principle!

Because of this particularism, nominalism paved the road for scientific research and the empirical attitude. This had dramatic implications for man's understanding of the world: the scientific mind began to cut reality into autonomous segments, each of them representing a field of specialized research in which inductive and quantitative rather than deductive and speculative methods are to be applied. As we will see in a moment, this empirical attitude has gradually rendered the sciences to a level of abstraction where methods supersede substance, and specialization impedes any kind of comprehensive knowledge.

Parallel to this diversification of knowledge ran the pluralization of society into many rather autonomous institutional sectors. The rise of the cities, the loss of socioeconomic power on the part of the nobility, the development of capitalism, technology and industry, and the religious diversification under the influence of the Reformation, gave birth to a highly complex, *pluralistic society*, based upon a new principle of organization. Medieval patrimonialism continued to dominate some of the institutional sectors of pluralistic society (namely those of religion, family, and education), but could no longer function for society in general. A subtle division of countless specialized functions, a large scale of various levels of rewards and status allocations, a differentiation of spheres of authority and power, became mandatory and had to be organized on strictly rational and efficient grounds. Rational *bureaucracy* fulfilled this task.

I have distinguished modern abstract, pluralistic society from ancient Graeco-Roman and medieval society where man still experienced his world as a structured *Gestalt* of which he himself was an inherent part, claiming that such an idealtypical comparison enables us to visualize the fundamental characteristics of our own world. I have also suggested that we compare our society to so-called "primitive" or developing societies. I would like to introduce at this point the *theory of the Common Human Pattern*, developed by the late Dutch historian Jan Romein.

If we do not hesitate to make idealtypical comparisons, Romein asserts, and liken twentieth-century Asia to Europe's past, we discover a striking similarity between medieval Europe and contemporary Asia. Moreover, if we compare these Asian societies to contemporary Africa and South America, we can again observe some strong similarities. This suggests that the not-yet-industrialized pre-modern civilizations of medieval Europe, ancient Greece and Rome, medieval Arabia, pre-modern Asia, Africa and America, constitute collectively one characteristic configuration which Romein called the *Common Human Pattern from which industrial Europe and northern America deviate*. This means not that the so-called primitive tribe in Africa deviates from industrial society, but that the latter deviates from the former. From the historical point of view, the African tribe is still a "normal" representative of the Common Human Pattern.[11]

Romein attributed the following characteristics to the Common Human Pattern (CHP): The CHP-man, as Romein called him, has a *subjective attitude toward nature*. He feels himself part of nature and thus cannot objectify it. This has implications for his attitude toward science and technology, both of which try to manipulate nature in an objective, value-free way. The CHP-man rather endures nature. His magic, I might add, is a form of manipulation, but it is a manipulation of powers that are inherent to nature and cannot be understood through objective knowledge. Moreover, he has no free access to nature since this is barred by countless taboos. His *conception of life* is part of a cosmic philosophy. That is, life is not something to be realized by the individual but a gift of god, gods, spirits, or fate. It is something that happens to you, and since outside this world nothing can exist, death is seen as only a transition to a different mode of existence.

The thinking of the CHP-man is not abstract in the formalistic and rational sense of the word, but concrete and pragmatic, loaded with impressions, mythical connections, magical and symbolic connotations. Consequently, he is unable to organize his life in a strictly goal-oriented way, because organization requires planning future acts and measures on the level of abstract thought. Planning maps out behavior in terms of abstract projections, which is a manipulation that cannot occur in the CHP frame of reference. Hence, CHP-man's social, political and economic structures are organically grown in a long process of tradition rather than rationally organized. The *time awareness* of the CHP differs equally from ours. The CHP-man lives in the here and now and neutralizes the stream of time in the myth of eternal return. Progress and evolution, common intellectual properties in modern society, are senseless concepts to him.

Authority is of crucial importance in the CHP. The authority of the gods, or the father, or the teacher, or the book (Scriptures, Koran) is the cornerstone of the CHP and will never be questioned. It provides the world with stability and shields it from the threats of chaos and anomie. Consequently, the rise of modern society as a deviation from the CHP may be viewed as one sequence of emancipation movements. The Humanists of the Renaissance (according to Romein the first to be aware of the near deviation from the CHP) rejected the authority of the Church while accepting a new authority by adopting the norms of antiquity. This, however, was an authority that for the first time in history had been chosen by free will. The Protestants of the Reformation refused to acknowledge the authority of the Pope but bound themselves to the authority of the Scriptures. The Enlightenment carried on the movement of the first Humanists, but rejected the authority of antiquity, exchanging it for a power from within: human reason as final authority. When at last this authority too lost its command over man, all authority seemed to have vanished. This seems to be precisely our present situation.

Romein mentions the *attitude toward work* as a last aspect in which the CHP differs from industrial society. To the CHP-man, work is always essentially viewed as a curse. With the rise of urban citizenry and their protestant ethics, work changed from curse to blessing (or at least obligation).

The obedient functionary was ready to appear on the scene, we might add.

Romein was the first to acknowledge that this picture of the CHP is a global one and calls for several differentiations. He therefore stresses repeatedly the idealtypical nature of the CHP concept, which draws its generality mainly from its deviation—Western, industrial society.

The theory of the Common Human Pattern, it seems to me, has a heuristic value for our concept of "abstract society." By comparing modern society with the CHP, its abstract nature receives greater emphasis. Modern man no longer experiences himself as constitutive part of a surrounding world. He is largely estranged from nature and endures his society as something that confronts him. He does not "live society," he faces it. The CHP-man, on the contrary, experiences even nature as a social community of events and objects that are near to him and belong to him (cf. totemism). He cannot separate himself from his social collectivity (clan, tribe) with its religious rituals and traditional institutions. These ties between man and his environment, strong as they were in the CHP, have been severed in the process of modernization. The individual has become autonomous and so has his social environment. (Chapter 5 will deal with this epochal phenomenon in greater detail.)

At this point, I must add one aspect to Romein's idealtype of the CHP. The social structures within a CHP society are inseparably interwoven and firmly rooted in the basic institutions of *kinship* and *religion*. As a result, the CHP-man sees society and the world of animals and things in terms of face-to-face relationships in which he participates with all of his being. He experiences his world as a closed configuration, a formed *Gestalt* (Guardini)—as a very familiar totality with sacred qualities. Thus, the stability of his identity is guaranteed by the stability of his world.

The stability and homogeneity of pre-industrial society, it must be noted, is of a *cultural* rather than *structural* nature. Or, in Durkheim's terms, the solidarity in the CHP societies is *mechanical* rather than *organic*. In his *Problems of an Industrial Society* (1968), William Faunce describes a small non-industrial community in the central highlands of Guatemala. The social structure of this village is rather undifferentiated. Status and power differences are minimal and everybody is generally doing the same kind of thing. Reciprocal role relationships such as employer-employee, buyer-seller, parishioner-priest, doctor-patient are almost nonexistent, since social relationships are more determined by the family unit than by the larger community. The dominant reciprocal role relationships are therefore virtually all within the family (husband-wife, father-son, etc.). Social isolation is consequently great. The fences between the households, for instance, function not only as physical boundaries but as social barriers as well. Close friendships are rare, and conflicts, though they occur regularly, are of an interpersonal but rather petty nature. "The villagers," says Faunce, "appear to feel that they can afford neither friends nor enemies."[12] The social structure is atomistic and shows little integration. However, the villagers are all united by a common way of life. Says Faunce: "In spite of interpersonal conflict and the relative social isolation of each household, there is a high level of consensus in the village regarding important values and attitudes, and there is very little behavior that is clearly deviant from the prescribed patterns. The lack of structural differentiation means that the (villagers) live under very similar conditions and share a common way of life."[13] Following Durkheim, Faunce describes these two different forms of integration as follows: "Mechanical solidarity refers to social integration resulting from the sharing of a *common culture* or way of life, and organic solidarity is integration resulting from *interdependence* in a structurally differentiated social unit."[14]

In the same context, Faunce mentions the lack of social change in non-industrial society. This, indeed, is an essential aspect that should be added to the characteristics of the CHP. I quote Faunce on this important point:

Extreme poverty, disease, a high infant-mortality rate, and illiteracy are characteristic of life in the village. Although the (villagers) would clearly rather be rich than poor and would prefer health to sickness, there is a kind of hopelessness and a fatalistic attitude toward these conditions.

They are facts of life in the village, and there are almost no systematic attempts on the part of the villagers to change them. The traditional ways of doing things are valued in themselves, and the connection between these traditions and the problems of the village are only dimly perceived, if at all, by the (villagers). Any concerted effort to introduce change from within the village is unlikely to occur because of its atomistic structure. Where there is no established leadership and no social organization above the level of the household, it is difficult for people to act together to resolve their common problems. Where these problems are perceived not as *social* problems requiring concerted action but as individual misfortunes or as intrinsic aspects of a hard but otherwise valued way of life, change becomes even less likely.[15]

We may draw the following conclusion from this: CHP societies are characterized by a high *cultural integration* based on "mechanical solidarity." Their *structural integration* based upon "organic solidarity" is generally low because of their undifferentiated social structure. Industrial societies, on the contrary, have a highly differentiated pluralistic social structure and their social integration tends to be structural and functional rather than cultural and traditional. The second part of this statement needs further elaboration.

Compared to the homogeneity of the CHP societies, industrial society displays a high amount of structural differentiation. This is particularly manifest in what Ralf Dahrendorf has called the *institutional isolation* in industrial society. This is the tendency of institutional sectors, such as the family, religion, education, government, the military system, etc., to grow autonomous. As autonomous sectors, they exert control over the individual only in so far as he falls within their "jurisdiction." As a result, industrial man must be able to adhere to partial allegiances. Family and religion, for example, are no longer the pillars upon which the total social structure rests and around which the individual organizes his allegiances. They are merely two institutional sectors next to many others, unable to exercise an exclusive control over the individual, as was normal in the CHP. Other sectors like science and industry took over their place, but the same thing has now happened to them. Industry in Marx's days, for instance, was still an overarching sector from which all social and economic processes could be explained and understood. Today, this sector appears as only one among many. Says Dahrendorf: "Industry appears as a society within society, a structural unit *sui generis,* which in a way is complete in itself without transcending its limits and without overlapping other structural units and associations."[16]

Dahrendorf's suggestive theory of institutional isolation, to which we will return in Chapter 5, seems to me to need a small correction. Comparing the institutional isolation of industry with the isolation of religion (the Church) can be misleading. The Church, the dominant institutional sector in the Middle Ages, is today admittedly just one sector among several. It is also true that industry has lost its dominant role in contemporary society and become structurally just another sector, relatively isolated from the others. But industry still determines almost every element of today's society, in a cultural way. The cultural outlook of Western society is "industrial" and "technological," as its arts, music and architecture and its pragmatic emphasis upon efficiency and rationality testify. Admittedly industry is no longer structurally dominant, but it penetrates all aspects of modern life from the cultural point of view.

This conclusion suggests an important theoretical consideration: institutional sectors can continue to dominate society at the cultural level after they have lost their predominance at the structural level. Today, it seems to me, the Church has lost its influence on man and society, both structurally and culturally, but it dominated Western society at the cultural level far longer than at the structural level. Two examples can support this assertion. Calvinist ethics continued to function as a cultural force (called the "Protestant Ethic") outside the institutional Calvinist religion and long after Calvinism had lost its structural importance as a Church. The second, related example is the "vague religiosity" of the American Way of Life as a cultural force that reaches far beyond the limits of America's institutionalized religion.[17]

Evidently, our pluralistic society with its chaotic amount of specialized, relatively isolated institutional sectors is badly in need of a coordinating principle. This need is satisfied by bureaucracy, a form of organization based upon rationality which has evolved into a highly formalistic structure. In a way, bureaucracy has taken over religion's unifying role, without, of course, being able to provide man with the meaning that religion could give him. We will return to this point in Chapter 5.

The individual in this pluralistic society encounters considerable problems in establishing his *identity*. While the CHP-man has his identity ascribed to him right after birth, modern man caught up in various partial allegiances is faced by many choices of identity construction. Living between various institutional sectors, each requiring from him a behavior that conforms to its autonomous norms and values, the individual will automatically develop a pluralistic identity. Naturally, the acquisition and maintenance of such a pluralistic identity puts a heavy burden on him. Moving between the institutional sectors, the modern individual is compelled to change roles like the jackets of his wardrobe. A distance grows between himself and his roles, and he experiences a loss of meaning and reality, which usually is called "alienation." Thus, if he identifies himself with the institutional sector of the Church with its particular norms and values, he experiences alienation upon entering the institutional sector of the army, which presents him with a totally different world; and if he identifies himself with this sector, he runs into similar problems upon entering the institutional sector of the university. He is still on the horizontal level of mobility between sectors. Naturally, vertical mobility on the stratification ladder adds weight to the problem.

In contrast to this, the CHP-man knows his place in the world; his society embodies a cultural totality of interrelated parts. Being born in a certain family, the individual in the CHP is predetermined to occupy a certain social level and to be trained in a certain profession. His marriage is prearranged: a girl is selected, often by the parents, from a limited and predictable group. It is, furthermore, improbable that his social position and status will be subjected to any remarkable changes during the course of his life. The stratification patterns of CHP-societies, if present at all, are firmly established and change very slowly. The mobility between the strata is minimal, if not absent as in the case of the Indian caste system. Man's social position and his identity are predictable and stable. Like his freedom, his identity is real by being absent as a problem.

Turning to modern society again, we get a totally different picture. A clear-cut stratification pattern that distributes class, status and power over concrete generally accepted strata, seems not to exist! Such uniform realities as caste, estate, or class, which give a society a strict structure, are conspicuously absent in pluralistic society. Together with the increase of differentiation goes a gradual *leveling of class differences,* resulting in a society with a rather uniform and predominantly consumptive style of life. The German sociologist Helmuth Schelsky, who has developed this theory, claims that the Marxian dualism of conflicting classes has changed into a situation in which industrial man, from worker to manager, feels threatened by an abstract reality, usually called "the system."[18] Such an abstract and leveled society does not, of course, have the power to form the identity of the individual coherently. The modern individual wonders what his place actually is within the still obvious inequalities of income, wealth, status and power. The world becomes vague to him. W. I. Thomas has formulated this very nicely:

The definition of the situation (in modern society) is equivalent to the determination of the vague. In the Russian *mir* and the American rural community of fifty years ago nothing was left vague, all was defined. But in the general world movement to which I have referred, connected with free communication in space and free communication of thought, not only particular situations but the most general situations have become vague.[19]

In this vague society, social roles tend to grow ever more autonomous, with grave implications for man's identity and morality. From being containers of freedom and reality, social structures and social roles grow into their exact opposite, become abstract fetters that mold modern man's actions, thoughts and emotions according to leveled and uniform patterns.

We can apply to this situation the sharp observation of the Austrian poet and novelist Robert Musil that a man without qualities consists of qualities without man.

Abstract Society and Modern Knowledge

Abstract society with its loss of totality and reality has changed man's traditional consciousness and knowledge. Compared to traditional pre-industrial man, modern man operates with an essentially different form of knowledge and consciousness. We experience, view and know the world differently. The process of modernization has not only changed the socio-economic and socio-cultural structures of society, but has also had grave implications for the epistemological and psychological constitution of man.

The rise of modern society as a deviation from the Common Human Pattern may be viewed as a process of expansion and differentiation. Modern society is an expanding universe leading to a highly segmented mass society ruled by industry, technology and science, and organized by the rational principles of bureaucracy.[20] Within the relatively autonomous sectors of this society (family, Church, education, government, etc.), new institutions emerged to cope with the ever-increasing demands of this expanding universe. At the same time functions traditionally allocated to one sector were being transferred to others or developed into new and separate sectors, as has happened in the case of education, which in the Middle Ages was taken care of by the Church and the family, but gradually developed into an autonomous sector. Within these sectors an increasing division of labor (specialization) became mandatory, which again increased the already established institutional complexity. In this way, an *internal pluralism* within institutional sectors accompanied the *external pluralism* between these sectors. Sectors divide into sub-sectors, functions into sub-functions, positions into sub-positions. The individual is required to construct a more or less coherent life span in this institutional labyrinth. It is a miracle that he has not got even more lost than he has. As a matter of fact, the majority, as we will see in the next chapter, conforms to the existing circumstances trying to construct, in a kind of *carpe diem* mentality, its private world from institutional bits and pieces. Others, numerically a minority, revolt, either through protest or through subjectivistic withdrawal.

This pluralism is particularly apparent in the realm of human thought and intellect. Surveying the intellectual scene of the past couple of centuries, we see several attempts to grasp all of human reality in a bird's-eye view. Auguste Comte's and Hegel's philosophies are probably the most conspicuous examples.[21] In a combination of Platonic metaphysics and Aristotelian comprehensiveness, Hegel constructed a grand theoretical system into which all of historical and natural reality had to be forced. It is, I think, appropriate to call this endeavor *intellectual totalitarianism*. And indeed, as a philosophical school, Hegelianism has always been sympathetic to totalitarianism, from the far left to the far right.[22]

According to Karl Marx, Hegelian totalitarianism was utterly unreal and abstract. He reformulated it in terms of socio-economic reality and thus carried on Hegel's search for totality and comprehensiveness. In Marx, the dialectical method, the Promethean attempt to grasp all of reality and history in a single scope, returns in socio-economic terms of conflicting classes. The final clash between these classes, i.e. the revolution and the victory of the proletariat, will herald the end of history and the beginning of the "realm of freedom" where a totally human and a humanly total community will be restored. The utopia of a communist society is the dream of a human totality experienced as meaningful and real. It is the paradise of freedom which man lost long ago.[23]

However—and this is crucial—until all of mankind has become faithful to the principles of Marxism, society has to be ruled dictatorially by the truly believing elite, organized in the party. This dictatorship is the still incomplete projection of a final, eschatological totality. It is the totalitarianism of Lycurgus in Sparta, Calvin in Geneva, Stalin in Russia, or Hitler in Germany. As different as their philosophies were,

Does Kuhn represent a counter-thrust?

they all were similar in one respect: their common intellectual totalitarianism was realized in society by terror and violence.

Intellectual totalitarianism can be viewed as a compensation for the loss of totality in everyday life, a search for a pseudo-totality that would restore a coherent framework of meaning, reality and freedom. The recent history of Europe has demonstrated what happens if this kind of theoretical totalitarianism is enacted politically. The totalitarian intellectual is usually a true believer who requires from his followers not just obedience but also conviction.[24]

A contrary reaction to modern pluralism is the *specialization of the sciences*. Whereas intellectual totalitarianism tries to impose totality on a fragmented reality, specialization seems to reflect the fragmentation. In other words, the modern mind has conformed to the pluralization of the world through specialization which cuts reality into little pieces, each piece being the domain of a relatively small group of experts. These experts discuss their theories within their own little group where they apply their own "secret language." Here they engage in research, and after their field has been exhausted, theories about theories are developed. Many of these specialties have become so abstract and obscure that not only colleagues within the same discipline but even experts within a single specialty have difficulty understanding each other's issues. This is the exact opposite of intellectual totalitarianism, and I propose to call it *intellectual Taylorism*.

It is important, however, to bear in mind that not only scientific knowledge has been segmented. A similar process has occurred in everyday knowledge, impeding normal everyday conversations considerably. W. I. Thomas has described it as follows:

> The world has become large, alluring, and confusing. . . . There is no universally accepted body of doctrines and practices. The church-man, for example, and the scientist educator, or radical leader are so far apart that they cannot talk together. They are, as the Greeks expressed it, in different "universes of discourse."[25]

Intellectual Taylorism has important implication for modern knowledge, in both its scientific and everyday aspects. I shall restrict myself to scientific specialization since the main trends of segmented knowledge are articulated there.

By cutting reality into small pieces, the scientist is in danger of losing all sense of reality. Sooner or later, many specialties and sub-specialties are doomed to be exhausted. The specialist is then compelled to focus on the refinement of existing theoretical models and methods, or to do research for the sake of research without actually adding much to the existing body of knowledge within the field. If one doubts this, one has only to browse through recent Ph.D. dissertations within various disciplines. Abstract formalism has generally superseded all substance—a process that is remarkably in tune with the main tenets of abstract society.

A second, closely related danger lies in the definition of reality that may result from specialization. The specialist and his small circle of co-experts are inclined to define their own little field (i.e. their specialized theories and methods) as the final reality or as *the* representation of total reality. Hardly in touch with other disciplines, the specialist suffers from professional blindness and endows the precarious constructions of his particular specialty with absolute and exclusive characteristics. The modern expert is a skilled operator who usually lacks the modesty one would expect from a conscientious worker in a limited and rather small field. In addition to this, he is mostly a naïve spectator in all matters that happen to transcend his little world.

This naïveté of the specialized intellectual has implications for his position in the modern world. He is often utterly helpless in confronting the many complex problems of today. If he is compelled to step outside his small world of expertise (for instance, under the pressures of student politics on the campus), he is apt to surrender easily to all sorts of ideologies. In short, what Werner Sombart said about the modern businessman also applies to the modern specialized intellectual: he gets nervous outside his field of expertise where he senses an awful feeling of emptiness.[26]

Arnold Gehlen made some important observations about the change in modern man's faculties of knowledge.[27] One of the most conspicuous aspects of the rise of technology (assisted by industry and the sciences) is, according to Gehlen, that the inorganic supersedes the organic and a cultural superstructure emerges in which the "big three" of modern society (technology, industry and science) rule. In this world of the inorganic, experiment and continuous abstraction seem to dominate. Modern man has substituted inorganic for organic material, and inorganic energy for organic power. A *nature artificielle* has spread out over the world.

Following Henri Bergson, Gehlen points to the fundamental similarity between the inorganic and man's rationality: both are conditioned by causality. Organic life will probably always remain a puzzling problem to man, but the inorganic is relatively easily accessible and can be manipulated. Hence, man tries to replace the organic by the inorganic as much as possible.[28]

Thus, a whole new world has developed, marked by machines, instruments, experiments, measurability, functionality, rationality and abstraction. This world is dominated by technology, science and industry. It is rationally organized by bureaucracy with its abstract and "inorganic" division of tasks, rights, obligations, and responsibilities. A relatively recent addition to this abstract world is the *process of automation*. Its influences on human labor and the structures of society have been sufficiently discussed. I want to stress here its profound influence on the knowledge of modern man. Whereas traditional man tried to understand his environment in terms of a kind of super-mind (the Greek *Logos*, or the Hegelian Spirit), modern man seems to operate the other way around. He does not compare the automatic machines to his mind, but applies cybernetic models and metaphors in order to get a better understanding of the nature and functions of the human brain. Today, the computer does not resemble the human mind, but the human mind operates like a computer. This, of course, does not keep us from referring to computers in anthropomorphic categories. However, these categories say more about our image of man than about automatic machines.

What was said above about the sciences can also be observed in modern music and modern arts. Here, too, totality and reality are conspicuously absent. Experiments and abstractions dominate. Monet experimented on his canvas with light, painting the same cathedral at different times of the day. However, this experiment still functioned as means for a goal. That changed with Mondrian. As a young painter, Mondrian developed the experiment itself into a standard painting technique. His highly abstract paintings are exercises in experimentalism (comparable to the heavy emphasis on methodology in the sciences). His monotonous variations of the same, exclusively primary colors in the same, exclusively geometric configurations are the final consequence of a world in which substance is superseded by forms, material by methods, essence by functions, reality by abstractions. Mondrian's world is pure, clean, rational, sterile, serene, measurable, and functional. Electronic music is another field in which experiments are end products. This music is abstract and disengaged from human emotions. Fabricated in laboratories (mostly equipped with the newest gadgets of electronic technology and subsidized by industry), electronic music is the product of experimentations with highly abstract formulas. It is cold and sterile, measurable and scientific, abstract like the paintings of Mondrian. The composer with his creative craftmanship is obsolete—he has been succeeded by the electronic engineer who is the skilled operator of formalized calculations that are fed to electronic tubes.

This rationality can easily turn into its opposite. That is the *mystique* of the empty canvas, the blank sheet of paper, absurd formulas thrown into madly running computers, theatrical madness and total absurdity. The final consequence of experimentalism is abstraction *ad absurdum;* it is madness or suicide. We see this today. It is called "art," but that is just a name.

Abstract Society and Modern Consciousness

The concept knowledge, as used in the former section, refers to man's understanding and representation of the world. The concept consciousness focuses more on man's general awareness of the world, which again directs his attitudes toward his environment. The two are to be distinguished theoretically only. In reality, knowledge is a part of consciousness.

Fundamental to Arnold Gehlen's philosophical anthropology is the notion that human consciousness underwent a qualitative change during the transition from traditional to industrial society, a change comparable in its impact on man's psychological constitution to the Neolithic revolution in which man changed from a hunting, nomadic existence to an agricultural, domestic way of life. The Neolithic revolution brought large settlements, differentiations in wealth, property and authority, the establishment of gods in temples and organized cults, in short, a total reorganization of life. In this epochal transition, Gehlen holds, man's consciousness must have altered fundamentally. During the rise of industrialism, social structures and human consciousness endured a similar qualitative change: "Comparably radical will be the change of the world by industrial culture, when man will weave a steel and wireless blanket around the world. We are still at the beginning of this process and in its first couple of centuries."[29]

Two aspects are typical of modern consciousness, according to Gehlen: on the one hand, an increasing *intellectualization;* on the other, a growing *primitivization.* By intellectualization Gehlen means the tendency to think and speak in terms of highly abstract models and formalistic categories, to experiment and to emphasize calculable effects. Parallel to this runs modern man's tendency to express himself in slogans. He has a need for simplicity and plasticity, and a concurrent aversion to subtle conceptual distinctions and nuances. He sacrifices intellectual honesty for popularity and emotional satisfaction. Gehlen calls this primitivization. It is represented by the mass media which continuously bombard us with their slogans and nervous shocks promising us the newest, the latest, the best and the deepest.

In this context, I must again mention Helmuth Schelsky's theory of the leveling of modern society. Industrial society is subjected to a leveling of standards, norms and values that were formerly bound to particular social layers but today float around like pieces of common property. To formulate this in my own terminology: the *grand seigneur* and the proletarian shake hands in a colorless culture that lacks the greatness and tragedy of the proletariat and the lavish *grandeur* of the upper classes. A cultural uniformity has spread out over industrial society which is coached and stimulated by the mass media that offer fads, fashions, norms and values by the thousands merely for the sake of consumption. The supermarket—clean, streamlined, ready-made and packed, uniform and functional—gives an adequate picture of this leveled culture of ours. It presents a perfect image of a consumer society.

However, modern man is not only a consumer in a uniform culture but also a functionary in a bureaucratically organized system that requires the *bureaucratic attitude*. The system needs detached and strictly functional experts—rational apparatchiks who are sufficiently dehumanized to be factors in the realization of calculable goals.

Applying Gehlen's notion of a qualitative change in man's consciousness during the transition from traditional to modern society, we may mention the bureaucratic attitude as a most important aspect. This attitude has become part of our consciousness. It influences all of us, even far outside the proper realms of bureaucracy. The village woman who is accustomed to shop in a small, local grocery store where she is served by the shopkeeper personally and discusses with him the latest gossip is at a loss in a metropolitan supermarket where her demands are no longer directed by her needs, but on the contrary dictated by an abundant supply. She now has to organize her shopping in a rational manner. She has to apply a kind of planning, small as its dimensions may be. When she pays the bill, there is no time for gossip or personal information. She receives, together with her purchase, a small slip of paper with a precise calculation of her expenses. The words "Thank You" are printed on it, more for the sake of public than personal relations. The shopkeeper, the focal point in rural face-to-face relationships, has been replaced by machines and anonymous functionaries.[30]

In summary, industrial society, losing more and more of its reality and meaning in the experience of man, tends to reduce him to a specialized expert and dehumanized functionary. If we interpret human life as extended between the two balancing poles of exteriority and interiority, we may conclude that abstract society reduces human existence to just one pole, that of exteriority. The result of this reduction has been adequately baptized by the social philosopher Herbert Marcuse as "one dimensional man."

NOTES

1. Joseph Gabel, *La Fausse Conscience* (Paris: Les Editions de Minuit, 1962). Cf. also Peter L. Berger, Stanley Pullberg, "Reification and the Sociological Critique of Consciousness," *History and Theory* 4:2 (1965) 198 ff.
2. Ernst Topitsch, *Vom Ursprung und Ende der Metaphysik* (Wien: Springer Verlag, 1958).
3. Mircea Eliade, *Cosmos and History: The Myth of the Eternal Return*, 1954, transl. from the French by W. R. Trask (New York: Harper Torchbooks, 1959).
4. Romano Guardini, *Das Ende der Neuzeit* (Würzburg: Im Werkbund Verlag, 1950), p. 13: "Beide sehen und, was noch wichtiger ist, empfinden die Welt als begrenztes Gebilde, als geformte Gestalt—bildlich gesprochen als Kugel." The Hungarian philosopher Georg Lukacs wrote: "Der Kreis, in dem die Griechen metaphysisch leben, ist kleiner als der unsrige: darum koennen wir uns niemals in ihn lebendig hineinversetzen; besser gesagt: der Kreis dessen Geschlossenheit die transzendentale Wesensart ihres Lebens ausmacht, ist fuer uns gesprengt; wir koennen in einer geschlossenen Welt nicht mehr atmen." Georg Lukacs, *Schriften zur Literatursoziologie*, ed. P. Ludz (Neuwied-Berlin: Luchterhand Verlag, 1963), p. 84.
5. Claude Lévi-Strauss, *La Pensée Sauvage* (Paris: Librairie Plon, 1962).
6. Cf. for a good description of the Greek tragedies: H. D. F. Kitto, *Greek Tragedy*, 1952 (New York: Doubleday Anchor, 1954).
7. H. D. F. Kitto, *The Greeks*, 1951 (London: Penguin Books, 1966), p. 7.
8. N. D. Fustel de Coulanges, *The Ancient City*, 1864 (New York: Doubleday Anchor, n.d.), p. 220.
9. Rudolf Bultmann, *Geschichte und Eschatologie* (Tuebingen: Mohr-Siebeck, 1958), pp. 16 f.: "Das geschichtliche Geschehen wird in derselben Weise verstanden wie das kosmische Geschehen; es ist eine Bewegung, in der in allem Wechsel immer das gleiche geschieht in neuen Konstellationen." The translation in the text is mine (A.Z.).
10. Cf. Paul Hazard, *La Crise de la Conscience Européenne* (Paris: Librairie Arthème Fayard, 1961).

11. Jan Romein, "Het Algemeen Menselijk Patroon," in *Eender en Anders* (Amsterdam: Querido, 1964), pp. 63–85. Cf. also W. F. Wertheim, *East-West Parallels* (Chicago: Quadrangle Books, 1965), pp. 6 ff.

12. William A. Faunce, *Problems of an Industrial Society* (New York: McGraw-Hill, 1968), p. 13.

13. *Ibid.*, p. 13.

14. *Ibid.*, p. 14. Italics by Faunce.

15. *Ibid.*, p. 14.

16. Ralf Dahrendorf, *Class and Class Conflict in Industrial Society*, 1959 (London: Routledge & Kegan Paul, 1963), p. 270.

17. Cf. Will Herberg, *Protestant, Catholic, Jew* (New York: Doubleday Anchor, 1955); Peter L. Berger, *The Noise of Solemn Assemblies* (New York: Doubleday, 1961).

18. Helmuth Schelsky, *Auf der Suche nach Wirklichkeit* (Duesseldorf-Koeln: Eugen Diederichs Verlag, 1965), p. 341.

19. W. I. Thomas, *The Unadjusted Girl*, 1923 (New York: Harper Torchbooks, 1967), pp. 81 f.

20. The German sociologist and economist Werner Sombart gave an impressive historical account of this process in his phenomenal study *Der Moderne Kapitalismus*, 3 vols. (Muenchen-Leipzig: Von Duncker & Humblot, 1916–27).

21. See for an interesting comparison of Comte and Hegel: Albert Salomon, *The Tyranny of Progress* (New York: The Noonday Press, 1955).

22. See the very illuminating study of Ernst Topitsch, *Die Sozialphilosophie Hegels als Heilslehre und Herrschaftsideologie* (Neuwied-Berlin: Luchterhand Verlag, 1967). Topitsch discusses this point in detail.

23. For the gnostic elements in Hegelianism and Marxism, cf. Ernst Topitsch, "Marxismus und Gnosis," in Ernst Topitsch, *Sozialphilosophie zwischen Ideologie und Wissenschaft* (Neuwied-Berlin: Luchterhand Verlag, 1961), pp. 235–71. See also Eric Voegelin, *Science, Politics and Gnosticism* (Chicago: Regnery, Gateway Edition, 1968).

24. Cf. Eric Hoffer, *The True Believer*, 1951 (New York: Harper & Row, 1966).

25. W. I. Thomas, *o.c.*, p. 78.

26. Werner Sombart, *Das Wirtschaftsleben im Zeitalter des Hochkapitalismus*, Vol. III of *Der Moderne Kapitalismus*, p. 28.

27. I am indebted for the following to Arnold Gehlen, *Die Seele im technischen Zeitalter*, 1957 (Hamburg: Rowohlt Verlag, 1962).

28. The Bergsonian distinction of the organic (or Life) vis-à-vis the inorganic is, of course, somewhat outdated. Modern biochemistry has gained much knowledge about organic life and may well be able in the near future to reproduce organic life artificially. What concerns us in the present discussion is Gehlen's point that the human mind and the inorganic share a simi-

lar nature and are mutually attracted by a kind of elective affinity.

29. Arnold Gehlen, *o.c.*, p. 24. The translation in the text is mine (A.Z.).
30. Cf. C. Wright Mills, *The Power Elite* (New York: Oxford University Press, 1959), p. 305: "The small shop serving the neighborhood is replaced by the anonymity of the national corporation: mass advertisement replaces the personal influence of opinion between merchant and customer."

4

THE SPIRIT OF PROTEST

Participation and Manipulation

Each society can be viewed as a system of communication. Not only ideas, values, norms, symbols, written and spoken words—the objects usually associated with the concept of communication—but also economic goods from food and tools to women and slaves are communicated among human beings.[1] For the sake of clarity, I will distinguish communication that entails a symbolic exchange from communication that assumes the form of economic exchange, but, it must be noted that this distinction is artificial, since both forms are often inseparable. In many primitive cultures, the exchange of bridewealth is simultaneously an economic affair and a symbolic communication. The same can be said of Veblen's "conspicuous consumption" in Western civilization.

Communication is the heart of human actions and interactions. As such, it is the most general form of social relationship. Actually, it is impossible to think of any human action or relationship that does not entail one or another form of communication. We send messages in everything we are doing.

Beyond the distinction between symbolic and economic exchange, we could distinguish within the former such phenomena as gesture exchange, communication of knowledge, values and norms, exchange of symbols, jokes, myths, legends, and communication of emotional experiences. All these forms can be further differentiated in regard to their intensity and proximity: the exchange of signals in modern traffic is one form of communication, the nightly pillow talk of a married couple and their love-making, quite another.

The common factor is mutual dependence. Feuerbach expressed this in his "altruistic principle," which we discussed in the second chapter. Or, as Mead saw it, in the process of interaction I anticipate the actions and reactions of the other actor by addressing myself as if I were the other actor. I internalize the communication process into my self through the encounter with another actor. This enables me to participate in the further communication process. The crucial point is that, because of this internalization, my participation receives a feedback, which again stimulates and directs my further communicative behavior.

This steering and stimulating principle of the feedback is particularly articulate at the level of what Mead called the "conversation of gestures." Walking on the sidewalk of a busy street an astonishing amount of (mainly automatic, unconscious) steering takes place among the pedestrians—and this solely on the gesture level. A slight gesture of the body of one pedestrian functions immediately as a sign for others to change their course. This change is fed back in its turn and functions as stimulus for the former to change or continue his direction. In this way a collision is prevented, and the pedestrians pass each other in a civilized manner. They "understood" each other without further reflection. Now, this precise network of gestures is crudely disturbed if an intoxicated man enters the scene. He is unable to steer himself through the street, and his unco-ordinated gestures send very confusing messages. They are internalized by the others but cause a kind of shock since no meaningful response seems to be possible. Nobody takes any risks. The bodies are steered around the drunk with a sufficiently large curve. In normal circumstances people can allow themselves to pass each other in much shorter distances, sometimes slightly touching the other bodies. Incidentally, after we have passed the drunk on the sidewalk, we will most likely exchange laughs or smiles. This laughter is usually a queer combination of real amusement and embarrassment.

Max Weber once gave the example of two colliding cyclists on the corner of a street as an illustration of the difference between "blind" and "meaningful" events and actions. The fact of collision itself is not a real human act. It is a coincident, a "blind" event, comparable to natural disasters such as floods or volcanic eruptions. But the attempt to prevent the collision, or, in the case of an accident, the exchange of curses or polite excuses are meaningful because subjectively intended. It is this meaningful intentionality that transforms movements of the body into social actions and interactions of persons. To this, the internalization of behavior as a cybernetic principle may be added: we are able to steer our actions in a meaningful way because we internalize the gestures and actions of others and feed them back in further communication—as in a spiral movement.

Participation is a function of this internalization. If man is no longer able to internalize actively, he will store up in his self meaningless, disconnected pieces of information—abstract images and empty stereotypes which are continuously reflected upon but do not stimulate any further communicative behavior. Moreover, in such a situation the actor will gradually lose the capacity to question or criticize the incoming information. He will slowly develop into an easy object for manipulation. Opinions are consumed passively and stored up in consciousness for abstract reflections.

Such a decline of participation is not just the result of communication disturbances on the part of certain individuals. In contemporary society its cause is *structural* rather than individual and psychological. This, to me, is the main tenet of C. Wright Mills's theory of the "public" and the "mass."

Mills constructs two extreme types, the "community of publics" (public) and "mass society" (mass), to explain some of the main structural features of modern society in which the mass media play such a dominant role. The public is the idealtypical realization of the classic theory of democracy, whereas the mass is characterized by lack of participation. In the latter, secondhand experiences are forced upon people as empty images distributed by mass media. In the public, on the contrary, opinions are created by discussions, and approximately as many people express opinions as receive them. These opinions can easily be made effective in action since they are not inhibited by the control of authoritative institutions.

The mass is "an abstract collection of individuals" (Mills) in which fewer people express than receive opinions. These opinions are distributed by the mass media, which to a certain degree are controlled by authorities. Not discussions but passive consumption of opinions dominate the mass structure.[2] In the public, people know each other and experience their life as part of the community that surrounds them as a real totality. They are not caught in this structure because they can transcend it "individually by intellectual effort, socially by public action."[3] And if necessary, members of a public can act upon the authoritative institutions and influence their further development and functioning. In the mass, people live in different *milieux* in which they are more or less caught. This society is a phantomlike structure whose members know one another only as the players of roles within certain milieux: "the man who fixes the car, the girl who serves your lunch, the saleslady, the woman who takes care of your child at school during the day." Mills then summarizes the predicament of man in pluralistic society: "Prejudgment and stereotype flourish when people meet in such ways. The human reality of others does not, cannot, come through."[4]

In such a society, democracy becomes increasingly problematic. Inherent to the notion of democracy is the idea that the individual together with others can influence the decisions made in society. Mills observes the following paradox in modern industrial (mainly American) society: on the one hand, the power of decision making is centralized largely in three main blocks (the military, the political, and the business elites), who impose their decisions on the rest of society; on the other hand, the members of society themselves are more and more dispersed over a pluralistic structure of various milieux.[5] In such a situation, man loses his sense of reality and gets caught in the stereotypes and secondhand experiences with which the mass media present him. Gradually, he loses his critical independence and surrenders to socioeconomic and political manipulations.[6]

More than a decade has gone by since Mills published *The Power Elite* (1956). Several of the trends he observed have now fully developed, others did not work out quite the way he envisaged them. This is not the place to draw the final balance. I rather limit myself to one specific point. There is a trend Mills did not discuss to its full extent which requires further analysis and interpretation. This is the rise of a radical protest against modern society with its mass structure. As a matter of fact, Mills hoped strongly for such a protest when he proclaimed the need for a New Left movement that would supersede the Old Left which, in his opinion, had surrendered to technological and capitalist society. He expected such a New Left movement to come from young intellectuals, in particular from students at colleges and universities. The sixties more than validated this expectation.

Democracy between Consensus and Discontent

In sociological theory, organization and disorganization are two paired concepts. A society in which everybody acted according to the norms and rules, in which nobody deviated in convictions and behavior, would be a perfect example of total organization. Such a fictitious society would be based upon the absolute consensus of the general will of all involved. Conflict would be conspicuously absent, and total stability would exist. Any form of social change, of course, would be lacking. Such a society, if possible at all, would just stay there like an eternal paradise or nirvana—without change, without conflict, without history.

A society, on the other hand, in which everybody played havoc with the established norms and values, deviating collectively from the traditional ways, would be an example of complete disorganization. Conflict and continuous change would characterize. Such an equally fictitious society would be some kind of ongoing revolution without any crystallization. It would possess neither real development nor any history. It would not be a society at all.

Both total organization and total disorganization are extreme types. In actuality societies move between these poles. Some may move in the direction of total organization and exhibit a totalitarian appearance, others may go through periods of disorganization and instability. But generally a society displays characteristics of both poles.

A state of almost total disorganization can occur for a short while, as in the case of revolutions or foreign invasions. A revolution, for example, will overthrow the status quo and may plunge society into a situation in which nothing can be taken for granted. But after a while, a new order with norms and values will emerge and bring society back from its anomic state to a position somewhere between organization and disorganization, equilibrium and change, consensus and conflict.

Total organization is a societal state that is hard to imagine. It would transcend the changes and conflicts of history. As a matter of fact, it occurs only in man's dreams and fantasies about a Utopia of absolute peace, freedom and harmony. Marx's Communist Community is such a Utopia: it is the end of history and the beginning of "the realm of freedom." There will be no clash of interests in Marx's "realm of freedom," no conflict, no alienation. It is the humanly total and totally human society founded upon complete consensus. Such a total view requires, of course, total devotion and loyalty. Discontent cannot be tolerated. Therefore, Marx's and all other forms of total Utopia are totalitarian and often deny the very principles they stand for. Visions of total organization and absolute consensus are inherently anti-democratic and have to rely on violence.

What then is democracy? There is no concise definition. Democracy, in my opinion, is a residual category: neither total organization nor total disorganization. It lies "somewhere" between the two poles. It refuses to acknowledge any kind of one-sideness and moves on a hazardous path between organization and disorganization, consensus and discontent. There are situations that call for the disorganization of revolution to liberate man from too much control and dehumanization. There are also times when the aspect of organization has to be stressed to prevent society from sliding off into chaos.

This means that democracy may endorse revolution, but it will refuse to do so for the sake of revolution, or for the sake of the establishment of a total organization. Thus it is always in danger of falling prey to opportunism; it easily lacks firm principles and evades harsh decisions. It may even unconsciously promote the status quo and lose its vigilance in regard to possible inhuman trends in society. These are the risks that must be taken if one wants to save democracy from anti-democratic absolutism.

There is a rather awkward problem involved here. What precisely are *the criteria* by which one decides to move in the direction of organization, or in that of disorganization? By which criteria does one in certain circumstances insist on order and in others opt for revolution?

One might answer: "When inhuman trends in society emerge, in the direction of either anarchy or alienation." But that, of course, is not a real answer. What are the criteria by which one judges the human or inhuman nature of certain societal trends? Pluralistic society has no coherent value system. Thus, no coherent criteria exist by which democracy can be defended. As a result, in modern society democracy is more or less at the mercy of countless, widely varying opinions as to what constitutes democracy proper and what a truly human existence actually is. In the final analysis, modern man has to face the old question of whether he is able to follow the hazardous road of democracy with the help of only immanent and profoundly varying values. Modern history has witnessed the recurrent breakdown of democracy. Perhaps we are posed for the theological question of whether modern man is not sacrificing his humanity by sacrificing transcendent values. Indeed, the death of God may well be the death of man!

The preceding comments on participation in the process of communication, and on the relative position of democracy between consensus and discontent present the theoretical background for our discussion of various forms of protest against modern abstract society.

Conformism and Privatism

It is not so much the rise of totalitarianism in Eastern Europe and Asia as the general decline of democracy in contemporary Western civilization that should strike us as the most alarming sign of our time.

Communication in the form of symbolic exchange in which opinions are not only received and consumed but also created and expressed is waning rapidly in modern society. The in-

dividual is, moreover, increasingly urged to conform to bureaucratic patterns of behavior. He has to play the obedient
role of functionary and to act according to the demands of
invisible authority structures. The majority of society does
not say "no" to this, but conforms and accepts its fate passively. In their increasing leisure time, these conformists withdraw into their own private world where they consume the
commodities of an affluent society and the ready-made opinions of the mass media. The many complicated socio-political
problems transcend their little worlds, are excluded from
their lives. Conformism and withdrawal into the private
sphere constitute a style of life that permeates all industrial
societies, either "free" or "totalitarian." They are forms of adjustment to a given situation. This adjustment is politically
forced upon the people of Eastern Europe, whereas it is more
socially inflicted upon the people of the so-called "free
world." The effects, however, are much alike! There is one
important difference: the people living under totalitarian regimes know more clearly than we do which forces are coerc-
ing them and which forces should be fought if this coercion
becomes unbearable. We, in our presumably free world,
hardly know how and where to fight the forces that limit our
freedom. We hardly even know what these forces are and
vaguely call them "the system."

Although we will focus in this chapter on the forms of *revolt against* abstract society, we must discuss briefly the
above-mentioned forms of *adjustment to* this society, namely
conformism and privatism. An almost classic picture of conformism was given by David Riesman's idealtypical concept
"other-directedness." It is a form of conformism that is more
than an outside adjustment to the actions and expectations
of others. As Riesman suggests, other-directedness is internalized by the individual and becomes part of his personality:
"the other-directed person, though he has his eye very much
on the Joneses, aims to keep up with them not so much in
external details as in the quality of his inner experience. That
is, his great sensitivity keeps him in touch with others on
many more levels than the externals of appearance and
propriety."[7] He has an insatiable "psychological need for ap-
proval"[8] and consequently a fundamental "fear of noncon-

formity."[9] The social location of the other-directed personality type is, according to Riesman, the urban, new middle class with its characteristic patterns of consumption.

Privatization is another form of adjustment to modern society. In his analysis of Germany's postwar youth, Helmuth Schelsky described the strong tendency to withdraw from complex social and political problems into a relatively small, private world. He called this tendency "privatistic" and, following him, we will use the term *privatism* to indicate a mode of adaptation whereby the individual withdraws from the public and social into the private spheres of life. Schelsky did his research mainly among working-class youth between fourteen and twenty-five years of age. He called this group "the skeptical generation." They conform to the larger structures of industrial society. There is no real opposition to such social duties as military service, and despite all their critiques most of the skeptical generation plan a career as functionary in the establishment. But all of this is done within the narrow fringes of their private world and in a skeptical mood:

> One will accept the unavoidable political duties and performances (one gets used to the duties of election and military service), and one will try to secure for oneself a bureaucratic job as functionary despite all the aversion against bureaucracy and its need for functionaries. The necessity of adaptation, therefore, precedes all other available antagonisms.[10]

The private sphere emerges in such a situation as a refuge from the overwhelming and demanding powers of society. The skeptical generation will not organize in protest groups when its private world is threatened, because it does not believe in organized actions and organized groups. This privatism is, according to Schelsky, not only a dominant trait of the postwar generation of Germany but to a certain extent characterizes the youth of all Western society during the late forties and the fifties.

At the end of his book, however, Schelsky claims that a new generation is emerging which bears features that differ considerably from the privatistic qualities of the skeptical generation. This new generation, Schelsky says, is *more emotional*. It has an often "explosive protest-character" and tries to provoke the established order of society and its authority structure. It does not withdraw into a private world where it conforms to the demands of society, but goes out of its way to protest "against the manipulated satisfaction of modern life and against society's untouchable pull towards conformity."[11] This vitalistic protest against society will increase with the growing consolidation of industrial society. With admirable vision Schelsky predicted in 1957 what is reality today:

> I expect a "secessionist generation" of young people, characterized by a wave of "meaningless" attempts to escape a quilted modern world that is based upon a manipulated humanity, a convincing security and a general prosperity.[12]

It must be possible, some thirteen years later, to finish this picture of the *secessionist generation* and its spirit of protest. Other-directed conformism and skeptical privatism are still important modes of adaptation today, but the modern spirit of protest, predicted by Schelsky, has developed into a style of life that needs further analysis and interpretation.

Three Types of Protest

During the sixties, a spirit of protest spread throughout industrial and bureaucratic society. By its very nature, it represents a complex and manifold phenomenon. A casuistic report of its various modes and moods would merely reflect this complexity and thus contribute little or nothing to a theoretical understanding of the peculiar phenomenon. I have, therefore, constructed *three ideal types of protest* which do not occur in reality in their pure form but represent three of the main aspects of the spirit of protest as it manifests itself in the exotic rituals of hippies, the marijuana parties of frustrated middle-class youth, the teach-ins, sit-ins, and love-ins, the occupations of university buildings, demonstration marches, etc. etc. The three types are Gnosticism, Anarchism, and Activism. These, it must be emphasized, are just names. The first two, for instance, do not coincide with any historical movements, but are names for certain aspects of modern protest that bear gnostic and anarchistic traits. I will describe each type briefly and assess them in the context of the homo duplex theorem.

In order not to complicate the discussion unnecessarily, I must omit the emancipation struggles of the last couple of decades. The Asian, African and South American revolts against colonialism and imperialism, the rising insurgence of America's poor, are essentially similar protests against the existing circumstances of modern society and its unequal distribution of social, economic and political power. The war in Vietnam and the riots in American streets are congenial in that they represent, each in its own way, a revolt against predominant relations of power. Although the present discussion will not cover these facts directly, I must ask the reader to see them as integral parts of the spirit of protest against abstract society. As a matter of fact, the war in Vietnam and the unequal opportunities in American society are for many revolutionaries of the activist type merely two examples of the total scene they are fighting.

Another preliminary remark must be made. The reader might get the impression that I overestimate the relevance of the younger generation in my discussion of the spirit of protest and might object with the often heard argument that youngsters in their transition from childhood to adulthood have always rebelled against established norms and values, powers and authority, duties and responsibilities. This argument is not totally devoid of truth. However, limiting its range to a certain age group may lead one to misunderstand the dimensions of the modern spirit of protest and dissatisfaction. Personally, I am convinced that the withdrawal into the world of psychedelic experiences, the rituals of hippie-like groups and the tumultuous rallies of radical students stand for *a much more general dissatisfaction* in contemporary society. Less flamboyant than many of the younger generations, many older members of society too experience the frustrating awareness of having to live in an abstract society that demands efficient functionaries and neglects the fact that man is more than the social puppet he has become. At bottom, we witness *a fundamental malaise of democracy* which far transcends the problems of certain age groups. But it is the secessionist generation and its ruthless criticism that has laid bare this malaise.

In addition to this, one could interpret the lavish protest of the secessionist generation in very general terms as a re-awakening of man's eternal revolt against all forms of objectivity. This means that the younger generation's spirit of protest represents something much more general and universal than a "normal" insurrection of adolescents. This rebellion is essentially born of a fundamental romanticism that shares many features of the philosophical and religious revolt against all objectivity, called *gnosticism*. Because of its fierce and tumultuous revolts, the sixties will be remembered as a neo-romantic and neo-gnostic decade. We will have to come back to this point later.

THE GNOSTICISTS

One of the central issues in Max Weber's sociology is the development of rationalization in Western civilization. It affected man's *Weltanschauung* ("disenchantment of the world"), his economic organization (capitalism) and his social organization (rational bureaucracy). Weber was haunted by the question of why this rationalization occurred in the Occident and not in the Orient. The answer has to be sought, he claimed, in the differences of religion. By establishing ethics, religion is bound to influence man's social, political and economic activities. This is, of course, not the place to discuss Weber's sociology of religion and its consequences for a theoretical understanding of such phenomena as capitalism, bureaucracy, authority, power and secularization. We must stick to our argument.

Whatever the origin of rationalization might have been, it is important to see it in connection with that other fundamental Weberian concept: *charisma,* the anti-institutional, non-rational power that makes a person extraordinary in the eyes of his contemporaries. Charisma can be found in a person irrespective of age or position, and it escapes all institutional structures and traditional definitions. It often functions in this capacity as a critique or even attack on established structures. The charismatic prophet, for instance, reveals the narrow-mindedness of the professional priests. He brings a new message, promising new freedom, reality and meaning. The prophets of ancient Israel, Jesus of Nazareth, Mohammed of Mecca and Gautama of northern India lived and taught outside the existing religious system, each of them preaching a new order in which man would be liberated from the traditional fetters of an institutionalized religion. In short, charisma escapes the ordinary routine and its power is experienced as extraordinary.

But soon enough, a routinization of charisma will set in, especially after the death of the charismatic leader. A successor has to be chosen who can continue the charisma of the master. Weber called this a change of charisma into its exact opposite: charisma is no longer an intrinsic quality of an extraordinary person but is now attached to a traditional position and profession. From personal charisma, it has changed into professional charisma (*Amtscharisma*). This routinization is a process of institutionalization and rationalization, because the charismatic leader turns into a rationally appointed professional priest or political leader and his charismatic movement changes into an institutional church or political organization with a strict division of duties and obligations, status and power. Charisma then has been ossified.

During the evolution of Western civilization, charismatic movements have emerged regularly. The prophets in ancient Israel, protesting against a routinized priestly religion, the gnostics in the days of the early Christian Church, searching for meaning, reality and freedom in the alienating chaos of the Hellenistic era, the monastic orders and the various sects in the medieval Church, the Marxists and the hippies in industrial society, are as many examples of human attempts to escape from the petrification process of institutionalization and rationalization. But they all share a common tragic fate: the charismatic movement they instigate is doomed to wind up in institutional structures with a rational organization, that is if it does not disappear altogether. Sooner or later all charisma is doomed either to turn into its opposite, or to fade away.

During their many ages of development, the civilizations of Occident and Orient have both explored various ways to escape from routinization and its inherent coercion. Among several, the "road inward" has always been most prominent. Despite his constitutional dependence on exteriority, man has always tried to withdraw from the outer world of nature and culture into his own subjectivity; he has always been attracted by the irrational abodes of his emotional nature where he remains irresponsive to stimuli from the outside and irresponsible to social rights and duties—in a sense "socially dead." The Indian nirvana is a perfect example of such a "social death."

Many techniques have been designed to enable man to follow the "road inward"—from religious mysticism to the artificial trip of psychedelia. Like Hellenistic man, many a modern individual thirsts for the meaning that overrationalized abstract society denies him. He is in search of charismatic experiences and believes that these can be found in his "deepest" subjectivity. Incidentally, as always in the history of the Occident, it is at this point that truth and redemption are sought from the Orient: *ex oriente lux*. The Indian guru, the techniques of Yoga, the cosmic mysteries of astrology, and the obscurities of witchcraft are the ingredients of a modern syncretism that does not differ very much from Hellenistic syncretism. It is believed to satisfy a desperate search for new meaning and new reality. Despite his lofty unworldliness, Maharishi Mahesh travels by jet to the chaos of Western society, where he and his musicians appear to be profitable products on an eager market. His is an exotic mystique which is interpreted as the charisma modern man has been longing for. This says nothing about the value of oriental philosophies, but it tells us a lot about the state of modern occidental civilization.

In our age of consumption, the road of the Indian guru can be far too strenuous—as was demonstrated by one of the Beatles who returned to England after four days of meditation training at the Ganges, because he could not stand Indian food any longer.[13] Easier and in better harmony with our present patterns of consumption is the so-called *drug culture*. It also promises a kind of nirvana where experiences of pseudo-ecstasy and pseudo-charisma reign. The rational is overwhelmed by extraordinary emotions and visions which actually replace the far too well known, overexplored and routinized sexual experiences.[14] Mystagogues of the Timothy Leary type play the role of charismatic leader, satisfying the demand for new leadership—a leadership of the extraordinary, irrational and non-organized sort. In this situation, *everything exotic or extraordinary acquires the label of charisma*. The revival of astrology is of particular interest here: it closes the initially open universe in which everything seemed to be possible. The *horoscope* gives man the comforting illusion that his place in the cosmos has been predetermined and is thus not the result of pure chance.

Thus floating on emotions and impressions only, man will need ever newer and stronger stimuli. Without the restrictions of institutional norms and values, i.e. without some form of institutional asceticism, human emotions are in danger of running empty. Ever stronger shocks must be invented. In a rather hysterical mood, man will begin to follow each fad that presents itself as extraordinary, or, in native language, "far out." The fad is followed as long as it stimulates, or as long as one "gets a kick out of it." Supported strongly by the consumption industry that flourishes with each new fad, these emotional searchers become the victims of a gradual *escalation of shocks*. If one kick is far out, the next has to be farther out. It is an ongoing attempt to escape routinization.

These then are the Gnosticists in our society. They are not protesting against war or social injustices—unless such protests bring thrills and emotional shocks. They withdraw from reality into one or another form of subjective nirvana. Meanwhile, their protest against alienation has gradually turned into a kind of capitulation to the forces of abstract society.

As Gilles Quispel, H. Ch. Puech and other specialists in the field of gnosticism have said, *the gnostics of all ages search for God (i.e. for utter reality, meaning and freedom) in the depth of their own souls*. Whatever one can attribute to the gnostic religion, this subjectivism seems to be its essential feature. Since it naturally rejects all limits and traditional parameters which to a certain degree always curb the operations of man's subjectivity, gnosticism stays open to all kinds of syncretism: in ever different configurations, gnosticism has always displayed a peculiar mixture of the exotic, the strange and the alien with the subjective and the emotional. It is an emotional revolt against an objective and rational world. Fundamentally, gnosticism is a romantic and erotic *Weltanschauung,* and a world religion (cf. G. Quispel, *Gnosis als Weltreligion,* 1952).

Despite its irrational nature, gnosticism has been rationalized in the Occident into more or less logical systems of thought. Examples can be found from Valentine to Goethe and Jung. In his remarkable study of gnosticism, Quispel mentions Jungian depth psychology as an example of modern gnostic thought.[15] This observation can be extended to Freudian psychoanalysis, as Eric Voegelin has done.[16] Freudianism performs a role in contemporary American society that bears the characteristics of gnostic redemption.[17] The suburban patient on his analyst's couch shares gnostic intoxications with his social adversary, the LSD-taker and the marijuana smoker. We observe here a peculiar coalescing of opposites in which suburbia and psychedelia shake hands. As we will see later, this is not the irony of fate but lies in the very nature of things.

The gnostic journey of the soul through the cosmos in search of the divine, original light is revived in the psychedelic trip and its cosmic visions. Documents of the psychedelic movement reveal a deep longing for utter reality, the sense of which has been lost in abstract society. The trip, as one of its adherents confessed, is not a withdrawal from reality but a search for a higher and more intense reality:

> My first psychedelic experience was triggered by 400 milligrams of mescaline sulfate. It did indeed induce a flight, but instead of fleeing from reality, I flew more deeply into it. I had never before seen, touched, tasted, heard, smelled and felt so profound a personal unity and involvement with the concrete material world. My psychedelically accelerated mind did not merely grasp the symbolic poetic import, the utter simplicity and truth of

William Blake's ecstatic vision: for the first time in my life I literally saw "the world in a grain of sand". My exponentially heightened awareness saw through the static, one-dimensional, ego-constricted, false front which is the consciousness-constructed reality of the everyday world. This was no evasive flight from but a deep probe into reality.[18]

Note the verbose exorcism so typical of all gnosticism ("psychedelically accelerated mind," "exponentially heightened awareness," "consciousness-constructed reality"). This bombardment of words, used by psychedelic poets and television commercials alike, has to serve the above-mentioned escalation of shocks. Normal words are routinized, words now have to be "far out" in order to shock us.

By their very nature, gnosticists reject any form of institutional rationality. Emotional shocks are substituted for reality, hallucinatory visions replace meaning, and freely floating experiences without any social involvement or responsibility are called "freedom." For the Gnosticist, there are no structures, no institutions and thus no limits.

This brings us to another aspect of the Gnosticist type of protest. It is a feature we will also encounter in the other types of protest. I call it *romantic absolutism*. The Gnosticist is in search for *utter* reality, *total* meaning, and *absolute* freedom. Every compromise is rejected. The modern Gnosticist longs for the absolute and the final, just like his Romantic brother in the nineteenth century. The latter went literally out of his mind to experience the absolute and the eternal. Timothy Leary has as the heart of his message: "it becomes necessary for us to go out of our minds in order to use our heads."[19] This is the romantic version of the *sacrificium intellectus,* for the sake not of faith but of emotional experiences.

What romantic absolutism leads to is illustrated by the fate of modern art. The superficial observer sees hardly any congeniality between the abstract art of Mondrian or Kandinsky and the lavishly Romantic paintings of Delacroix. However, after closer scrutiny, Mondrian and Kandinsky appear as the final consequences of nineteenth-century Romanticism and its search for utter reality. Mondrian, probably the most gnostic painter of this century, reached the last possible stage of Romantic nostalgia for the absolute and the eternal by stripping off all contacts with the outer world. One might call him the Edmund Husserl of art: he has reduced reality to the essence of basic lines and primary colors. Mondrian's art is a gnostic nirvana, neither cold nor hot, neither flesh nor blood. It is a world of pure aesthetics, as beautiful as a white piece of linen or an unwritten page of paper. His absolutism leads to the annihilation of art.

Mondrian was a mystic. However, Romantic absolutism can also be expressed in frenzied expressionism. *Dadaism* is a good example. It began in 1916 in Switzerland as a movement of young artists who were determined to liberate art from all limitations, in particular those of rationality and form. Unconditional freedom for the individual artist was Dada's goal. Its philosophy was absolutist and became increasingly nihilistic, anarchistic and eventually violent. Its essential feature was total opposition to everything, including Dada itself! A French dadaistic pamphlet said: *"Les vrais Dadas sont contre Dada"* (True Dadas are against Dada). This, again, illustrates the suicidal nature of Romantic absolutism and radicalism. It is also precisely this absolutism that brings the romantic rebel to a coalescing of opposites. *Pop art,* for example, consciously promotes kitsch to art. It is impossible today to distinguish the plush kitsch of suburbia from the products of pop art in a museum.

It is important to realize the political consequences of this romanticism. Emotions not sustained by institutional structures easily turn in all possible directions, like the weathercock on a tower exposed to different winds. The human being who floats on his emotions only stays open to many forms of manipulation. He may eventually be used for goals that entail sheer aggression and hatred. The increase in violence today has, of course, many causes. Romantic absolutism may be one of them. This needs further qualification.

Fascism in its most demonic appearance got hold of a country where overinstitutionalized discipline and coercion were paired with a very deep-seated romanticism: the Germans of the thirties, economically bewildered, culturally uprooted, politically and nationally wounded, were perfect material for Hitler's Third Reich. Such a configuration of factors will probably never occur again, but fascism as *the* Western disease, born of the paradox of rational organization on the one hand and irrational romanticism on the other, is apparently still omnipresent today! The overorganized rationality of abstract society paired with the romantic nostalgia of its members can only promote the fascist potential in our culture. If, in addition, this romantic nostalgia is combined with socio-political indifference (as in the case of many Gnosticists), or with sheer ignorance (as in the case of many conformists), we may well expect an increase in fascist seductions.

Not all members of the younger generation are socially and politically indifferent Gnosticists. There is a fundamentally different type of protest. Although these protesters may share many gnostic traits, they do not revolt primarily against rationalization and routinization, but against the existing authority and power relations of the established adult world. They too rebel against the petrified traditions of institutions, but not for the sake of romantic ecstasy. They aim at the renewal of reality, meaning and freedom within the framework of socio-political reality. They are politically very much involved. I call this group the Activists. They are actually the opposite of the Gnosticists.

But before we discuss this type of protest, we must turn to another type, the Anarchists. They occupy a position between the Gnosticists and the Activists; some of them have more gnostic, others more activist characteristics.

THE ANARCHISTS

A certain amount of anarchism is inherent to all forms of gnosticism. This is understandable since a retreat into man's inner world presupposes some kind of aversion to the outer, socio-cultural world. If this anarchistic element develops from individual gnosticism (e.g. the lonely drug consumer) or an elite mystery cult (e.g. Leary's LSD movement in its earlier days) into a subculture with an outspoken life-style and its own set of values and norms, we must distinguish analytically between two separate forms of behavior: beside the Gnosticists who protest against rationalization and routinization, we place the Anarchists who rebel against the traditional values of modern society. They launch an anti-culture (or perhaps better, a counter-culture) with its own specific style of life that denies everything holy to "straight" society. They take protest against rationalization for granted and rather focus on a revolt against the so-called Establishment and its institutional norms and traditional values. These Anarchists display a colorful, exotic and vitalistic life style in which, next to the drug scene, the return to nature, to "natural people" (e.g. the American Indian), to simplicity (love) and to magic (flower power) is advocated. As I have said, they usually exhibit all the features of the Gnosticists: Leary is the admired guru for many of them, Allen Ginsberg their verbose exorcist, and the music and philosophy of India an esoteric means for the experience of mysterious intoxications of sorts. They are, nevertheless, a different idealtypical group: they are primarily driven by an almost messianic desire to bring modern culture back to nature, to simplicity, to play and fun. Not all of them take drugs for "consciousness expansion," but they all do profess the style of life of the *homo ludens,* of the happy, nonfunctional, childlike individual who loves weird outfits and esoteric customs. In contrast to the rather grim existence of the modern functionary who is persecuted by his working ethos and obeys the demands of bureaucratic and abstract organizations, the hippie plays the flower child who enjoys bright colors, *Jugendstil* posters, and sentimental songs. Instead of political and socio-economic power, the flower child favors flower power with its irrational but fascinating magic. This is a counter-culture set up as a negation of our streamlined and "straight" society in which people work like uniformed apparatchiks under a continuous stress of societal demands, in search of ever more status and prestige. This counter-culture is an anarchistic denial of the norms and values of the Establishment, its social structure and its cultural style of life. It is, of course, anarchistic in the cultural, not the political sense of the word.

The Anarchists, as I said before, occupy a position between the Gnosticists and the Activists. Many of them drift away to the seductions of psychedelia and become the successors of the beatniks of the fifties. They are retreatists and refuse to accept any cultural or social responsibilities. Theirs is no longer a vision of a new culture with new meaning, reality and freedom. They have floated away on the subjectivistic waves of their emotions. Others, less introvert, organize magical rituals (e.g. love-ins, ceremonial burials, and other happenings). Or, in a sectarian mood, they withdraw from society and return to nature. Tolstoi's Jasnaja Poljana or Thoreau's Walden become models for hippie communes, one of which (near Los Angeles) bore the appropriate name Sans Souci Temple. These communes, often short term experiments, are located in nature, remote from urban civilization. They are based upon anarchistic communism in matters of economy and sexuality. Total liberty is called "freedom," and magical rituals are supposed to provide the members with meaning and reality. Rousseau's "happy primitive" has been resurrected too: the American Indian is the symbol of the naturalistic way. Some hippies organize in tribes, wear Indian costumes and carry talismans.

The Anarchists oppose not only the middle-class working ethos, but also the throat-cutting competitiveness of capitalist society. A sentimental philosophy of love is their alternative to this competitive way of life. Many of them go out of their way to be nice to each other and to outsiders. Far from being bomb-throwing political activists, these Anarchists put all the emphasis on peaceful resistance to cultural influences. Their philosophy of peace is couched in religious syncretism: Buddha, Christ, Gandhi, the child and the flower are its powerful and magical symbols.

The Gnosticist type of protest lacks the unmistakable cultural involvement of the Anarchists. The latter, however, are to be distinguished from the Activists. The Anarchists engage primarily in a *cultural* protest, whereas the Activists concentrate on *social and political* renewal. The former stress love, the latter do not shun acts of violence. But again, no sharp dividing lines occur in reality. The students of the New Left certainly envisage a reconstruction of cultural life; many Anarchists have been involved in political demonstrations. But there is an essential difference of emphasis, which was nicely illustrated by the typically anarchistic movement of the Provos in the Netherlands. It started as a hippielike group in the early sixties but became gradually involved in socio-political actions, without, however, ever becoming an Activist movement like the New Left. Let us have a closer look at this interesting group of Anarchists.

Born of a diffuse mixture of apolitical Gnosticists (mainly anti-cultural dropouts playing with magical rituals), the Provo movement gained its real dimension in Amsterdam sometime in 1962. It had its own philosophy with a peculiar, rather paradoxical attitude toward modern technological society: Provo rejected technology and urbanization in an almost reactionary manner, yet it remained typically urban and awaited the realization of its Utopia from the process of automation. Although psychedelia had a definite impact on Provo, its visions and dreams were of a socio-philosophical nature. Provo's Utopia was the New Babylon—a white city with white houses and white bicycles, without cars and factories and polluted air. Most important of all: New Babylon was to be the city of playing people who have fun together while automatic machines and cybernetic instruments do the work. Provo's anthropological model was *homo ludens,* and it was determined to realize this model despite all opposition from the Establishment. The Provos sought to prove that the Establishment was the prime cause of the corruption of man as homo ludens. The Establishment requires bureaucratic and functional obedience. Its demands are imposed by strictly authoritarian structures which leave little room for the creation of the free homo ludens. These structures are abstract and therefore hardly show their true, i.e. repressive and dehumanizing features. Thus the Establishment has to be constantly provoked so that it finally will reveal its true nature. Provocations became the technique of these Anarchists, and they drew from them their name.[20]

Provocation of the Establishment was only part of their program, however. The awakening of a "provotarian" consciousness among the younger generations was another aim. The worker class was viewed as being hopelessly entangled in the ties of "straight" society and thus unable to produce any real Provos. Future Provos were to be recruited among the "skeptical generation," that is, among those who hang around on the streets not knowing what to do with their leisure and money—dropouts, members of motor gangs and all sorts of misfits.

In a remarkably inventive way, the Provos of Amsterdam, calling themselves the provotariat, began their play with the established authorities. The Royal House, the Mayor of Amsterdam and, of course, the Police were viewed as the main symbols of an allegedly archaic and patriarchal society. They became Provo's main target. A periodical, simply called *Provo*, was published in which the reader received many suggestions for civil disobedience. The authorities fell in the trap and slashed back in a conspicuously humorless way, thus proving themselves unable to live the life of homo ludens. Issues of the periodical were confiscated and provotarian authors arrested for alleged incendiarism. In short, the authorities did precisely what the Provos wanted them to do: they proved what the Provos had claimed about them, namely that they are unable to play and thus pervert the homo ludens in man.[21]

The moment grew in size and attracted many sympathizers —and inevitably also a rather large number of "professional rioters" who protested for the sake of protest and provoked for the sake of provocation. National and international mass media displayed a rather dubious interest in the actions of the Provos. Incidentally, a traveling agency hired students who were disguised as Provos with the help of wigs and Provo-like attire to hang around in a certain district of Amsterdam where they were looked at by American tourists who bought tickets by the busload for the excursion, called "Visit Amsterdam's Provos." This says something about the commercialization of the spirit of protest.

The situation in Amsterdam grew tense as March 10, 1966 approached. It was the date set for the marriage of Princess Beatrix and Claus von Amsberg. Von Amsberg's German nationality and his service in the Wehrmacht during the Second World War caused strong resentment in Holland. A conflict situation arose in which everybody anxiously waited for the expected turmoil on the tenth of March in Amsterdam where the wedding would take place. This situation was, of course, highly favorable for the Provos, who, however, were opposed to this marriage more for provotarian than political reasons. They scared the authorities by announcing all kinds of disruptive actions during the wedding ceremonies. As a result, Amsterdam looked like a besieged citadel when the long awaited day finally began. It was meanwhile forgotten that play and not violence was Provo's goal. An admirably restricted protest took place. Several homemade smoke bombs were thrown at the thoroughly trained horses of the royal coaches and one Provo let a white chicken loose in the midst of the cavalcade. The horses did not react and followed their conditioned path. Something else happened instead: not the royal cavalcade but millions of television viewers at home and abroad were disturbed. The pictures were badly distorted by provotarian smoke—an inventive revenge against the hated communications media!

Not much attention was paid to the jocular way in which these provocations took place. Certainly not by the authorities who totally misapprehended the intentions of the jesters.[22] The Provos were usually called "subversive elements" and "dangerous anarchists" ("with no respect for law and order," of course). Hardly one of those in power was willing to consider the legitimacy of a great portion of Provo's criticism. None of them was willing to see himself as essentially a homo ludens. Violence finally broke out.

It was those "professional rioters," the press, the authorities and their police, who mainly caused a situation in which the Provos were compelled to play the role of Activists involved in a serious battle. It was the end of their joking. Under pressures of New Left elements, some Provos even founded a party which participated in the elections of the city of Amsterdam. It thereby entered the ranks of the Establishment as an opposition party. The end of Provo as an anarchistic movement was near. The Anarchists had become Activists; and they did not like it at all. Remaining loyal to their initial philosophy, Provo's death was "officially" announced in 1967.

The story of Provo illustrates the difference between the Anarchists and the Activists. Despite many gnostic elements in their philosophy, the Provos were more related to the Activists than to the Gnosticists. Yet they had a distinct character compared to the students and intellectuals of the New Left who are involved politically in an often violent revolt against the power elites of abstract society. We now turn to this third type of protest.

THE ACTIVISTS

Again, the activist type of protest does not occur in reality in a pure form. Many Activists exhibit gnostic and certainly anarchistic features. However, their main objective is not the experience of emotional shocks, or the realization of homo ludens, but the transformation of the socio-political and economic structures of modern society. They are deeply concerned with the role of modern intellectuals in the further development of Western industrial society and its relations to the Third World. Driven by Marxist notions, the Activist feels that revolutionary change has to be initiated by politically involved intellectuals since the working class has forsaken its calling as holder of revolutionary consciousness and praxis. But intellectuals, Activists claim, have been emasculated by the functional demands of our bureaucratic society. Instead of taking a critical stance, they have often conformed to this society. Activism is thus primarily a movement of younger intellectuals (mainly students, younger faculty members and artists) who have promised to restore intellectual relevancy in a society where neutral and inhuman forces of power rule.

In this frame of reference, all authority is by and large equated with power and dehumanizing coercion, and the end of all authority is called for. The Activist revolts against an amorphous "power elite," an "irresponsive system," and aims his criticism at the social and economic injustice of national and international poverty, at the political injustices of unequal rights and war, and generally at everything related to the power structure of "the Establishment"—whatever that may be. For this aim, intellectuals have to be mobilized, but, the Activist claims, they are hopelessly caught in the irrelevant structures of a traditional university which keeps faculty and students in a state of futile tutelage enacted by administrative authoritarianism. Therefore, the mobilization of the intelligentsia requires a fundamental reformation of the existing university system. As a result, the university has become the prime target of Activist protests.

The means applied by the Activist are not gnostic intoxications, anarchistic jokes or other forms of symbolic nonconformism, but well-planned, organized and often violent demonstrations. Sometimes, the protest remains restricted to non-violent strikes or campus sit-ins. Often, however, Activism transcends the boundaries of the university and is brought to the streets where a confrontation with the police—the hated symbol of Establishment power—is unavoidable. Meanwhile, the university administration and the government of the nation are usually equated as two elements of the same enemy. In Washington and San Francisco, Amsterdam and Berlin, Prague, Seoul, Tokyo and Djakarta similar protests have been organized on streets and campuses with the same kind of defiance. Gnosticism and Anarchism could eventually still be dismissed as excessive deviations of rebel rousing youngsters in search for their position in the adult world, but the Activists and their organized radicalism have brought the spirit of protest to the direct attention of those in power. Activists are not to be neglected politically, as many a powerful man from Clark Kerr to President Sukarno can testify.

Like Gnosticism and Anarchism, Activism has gradually moved in the direction of absolutism. Many Activists today profess the end of the university rather than its reform and preach unlimited destruction of "the system" instead of a revolution for the sake of a new society. In the late sixties, Activism grew increasingly irrational, thereby denying its intellectual origin. But let us first examine the kind of knowledge sought by the Activist prior to his later radicalism and irrational absolutism.

To begin with, one can observe among Activists, say in the days of Berkeley's Free Speech Movement (1964), a strong desire for new intellectual leadership. This role, they claim, can no longer be fulfilled by the intellectuals of the university since they are inhibited by both administrative authoritarianism and the methodological limitations of their disciplines. Let us focus on the latter aspect.

By its very nature, the university generates knowledge that is limited by the methodological demands of science. Not every kind of knowledge is permissible within its parameters. All statements of faith, to take a simple example, belong to religious organizations and are to be barred from the university as much as possible. The same can be said about statements born of political convictions. Today, however, young intellectuals call for existential rather than scientific, involved rather than theoretically detached, concrete rather than abstract knowledge. Methodological discipline is disregarded (like every form of discipline) and traditional logic is rejected as being largely sterile. They express contempt for the objectivity of the social scientist and admire sloganlike impressions which are easily accessible and stay open to different interpretations and manipulations. The impressionistic, associative, sometimes inventive, sometimes platitudinous theories of a Marshall McLuhan or the Hegelian-Marxian-Freudian world view of Herbert Marcuse are enthusiastically received, rarely understood, but eagerly manipulated. They satisfy an apparent desire for journalistic knowledge and *intellectual shocks:*[23] today, theories and philosophies have to be new, unheard of, thrilling and revealing. The intellectual needs of this generation are mainly irrational and emotional. And since a basic historical awareness is lacking, very few people seem to see that most new theories are neither new nor original. The Activist wants knowledge that can be applied and manipulated politically. He considers the painful "search for truth" as outdated, if not as nonsense. In this respect, he is as pragmatic as his adversary, the specialized scientist who silently conforms to the major values of American society. We are confronted here again by a peculiar coalescing of opposites.

The traditional university professor is, of course, not able to satisfy this need for existential (or relevant) knowledge. His place is taken by the popularizer who sweeps his audience with slogans and historically empty concepts. He will usually enjoy a short period of intense fame and achieve a world-wide distribution of one or two of his books. The phenomenon of the best-seller, unknown in the days of solid scientific work, is in this respect an indicator of the spirit of the time. The popularizer is admired by the thousands (although nobody seriously studies him) and the mass media, always eager to report new shocks, launch him jubilantly while comparing him with the greatest names in history. But after everyone has come to know him, he will be dropped. The reason for this is simple. The popularizer is unable to satisfy his audience with new shocks all the time. In search of the newest and the latest, his admirers are victims of an *escalation of intellectual shocks*, comparable to the escalation of emotional shocks, discussed earlier. No popularizer is original and creative enough to keep up with the demands of this escalation. After people have gotten to know him, he will be delivered to oblivion. They have already adopted the next intellectual fad. McLuhan and his *The Medium Is the Massage* (1966), an intellectual hit for almost a year, recently suffered the same fate as Bishop John Robinson and his *Honest to God* (1963): after a relatively brief period of worldwide fame, the bishop was dropped, like a toy thrown away by spoiled children who have played with it too intensively. Some had issued warnings, but they were brushed aside as being conservatives, comparable to those who objected to the revolutionary theories of Newton, Galileo, or Freud. This, incidentally, leads us to the formulation of the following law of modern thought: *Everything unusual is potentially radical; everything radical is morally good.*

The escalation of intellectual shocks implies, of course, a growing radicalization and an increase of absolutism. What was radical yesterday is conservative today. For instance, after we all were urged to be honest to God, a "new theology" preached the "death of God." This radicalization is successful because of the moral blackmail involved in the abovementioned law: nobody dares to be non-radical, since nobody wants to be regarded as immoral. Meanwhile, this radicalization in the modern spirit of protest leads eventually to selfliquidation. To resume the theological example: after the alleged death of God, a retreat to emotions seems to be the only alternative left for the modern theologian. Instead of preaching an often unpleasant message, the priest takes up the guitar and sings for his audience sentimental songs of love and loneliness. The audience appreciates the shock, but will return after a while to the Beatles and real soul music.

The protest against intellectual irrelevancy does not focus

exclusively on the type of knowledge fostered by the university. It concentrates as much (and even more flamboyantly) on the existing authority structure of this institution, as several revolts from Berkeley and Columbia to Berlin and Frankfurt testify. The university, one should remember, was originally an institution to train students in a scientific discipline in relative seclusion from society. The monastic order with its discipline and asceticism must have been an important model for the first universities. As much as the individual may be or has to be involved in the affairs of society at large, within the university the scholar has the privilege of approaching reality in a methodical and detached way. Thus, the scholar is in principle liberated from the many pressures of the outside world: the economic pressures of production, the political coercion of the state, the moral pressures of world views and religion. This relative liberation from social and political responsibilities was admittedly abused in the nineteenth century by the upper classes in order to defend their privileged position in society. It has been equally abused in the twentieth century by the middle classes in order to forsake their responsibilities to society. But these abuses do not invalidate the principle. The university is an institution that relieves the scholar, student and teacher alike from the pressures and responsibilities of daily life in order to approach reality in a methodical and detached way. This is of particular interest to the humanities, to which, in my opinion, the social sciences belong.

Within the parameters of the university, the social scientist as scholar is bound primarily by the disciplined rules of science. He is subjected to what might be called intellectual asceticism, not in order to be kept in spiritual tutelage or to deny his responsibilities as a member of society, but for the sake of rational and analytic knowledge which serves humanity only *indirectly*. The traditional idea of the university as an institution of open inquiry saves the scholar from the heated battles of philosophies and ideologies. As a living member of society, the scholar will get involved in these battles and eventually have to take a stance, but the university is the only institution in society that does not require this involvement. Its main function is to create room for open

inquiry and genuinely democratic discussions. Tolerance is
its very nature. It is also its vulnerable spot!

Participation in this institution requires a kind of restraint.
But restraint is a difficult thing to ask for in an emotional
and consumptive age. The modern individual longs for existential knowledge and demands political and social involvements. He is constantly at odds with the university on two
levels: its administrative hierarchy is accused of authoritarianism, and the knowledge it professes is viewed as being
irrelevant if not sterile. The Activist's conflict with the administration is more spectacular and gets therefore more pub-
licity, but the conflict with the standards of scientific knowledge is probably far more important, since a victory on the
part of the Activists in this case might entail the end of all
scientific work, particularly in the humanities. It would clear
the road for journalists and clairvoyants who would deliver
the humanities to series of short-term fads and fashions. The
humanities, abandoned to intellectual shocks, would be
doomed to become part of the pluralistic chaos they should
analyze and decipher. This would lead to an unintended conformity in the values and standards of modern industrial society.

At this point, we must bring into the discussion more
specifically the *growing radicalization of Activism*. In the days
of the Free Speech Movement at Berkeley, Activist students
were still very much occupied by the dilemma of open inquiry and active involvement. Being impatient with the state
of affairs in capitalist society, they cried for "involved" knowledge. They viewed the university as the breeding place for
the future functionaries of a repressive society. They were
seen as radicals in 1964. But what was radical yesterday is
conservative today. Absolutism has driven Activism beyond
its original objectives. At the end of the sixties, the question
of knowledge had become obsolete. The emphasis was increasingly placed upon a confrontation with the university's
authority structure and upon the increase of student power.
In the administration the Activist finally found a concrete
representative of the amorphous "system." Without further
reflection, administrations were defined as being "fascist," and
violence became by and large the device for giving meaning

to the cry for "student power." We must look at the various stages of this process in more detail.

In view of the Free Speech Movement at Berkeley, one should ask a very fundamental question in order to do justice to its protest: Does the modern university offer its scholars, students and faculty alike, room for the pursuit of knowledge in open inquiry, or has it become a factory that produces the functionaries, managers and technocrats for the future industrial society? Many of the Activists of those days believed firmly that the American university, always more enchanted by the pragmatic notion of a service institute than its European equivalent, prepares its students for societal conformism. Indeed, their cry for existential knowledge and their fear of scientific objectivity (as wrong as they may have been from the methodological point of view) must be understood as a critique of a university that assumed all the bureaucratic and functionalistic features of modern society. This point comes out very clearly, according to them, in Clark Kerr's vision of the multiversity which allegedly advocates surrender to the principles of technological society.[24] In an analysis of this pragmatic view of the modern university, three students summed up their criticism of Kerr as follows:

> Yet there is at least one idea that still survives in our society, although it has been part of our civilization for more than 800 years. That ideal is a university, a community of scholars bound together by the search for knowledge and truth, and feeling responsibility to their society. That ideal declares that teaching and learning are more important than economic self-interest, and where that ideal has been a reality, some men have been able to face the future with self-confidence and hope.[25]

These words are rather remote from the violent language to be heard in later stages of student radicalism, in which praxis has been severed from theory again (after their unity had been demanded): that is, theory is increasingly pushed aside by praxis. Radicalism has become mere Activism with the "barrel of the gun" as basic principle.

The protest of the Free Speech Movement was, of course, more than a philosophical debate on knowledge and educa-

tion. It was, in a wider sense, a revolt against the bureaucratic attitude of administrators. Mario Savio, one of its
leaders (whose radicalism is called "liberal" today) has
stressed this point many times. A famous statement of his is:

> Last summer I went to Mississippi to join the struggle there
> for civil rights. This fall I am engaged in another phase of
> the same struggle, this time in Berkeley. The two battle-
> fields may seem quite different to some observers, but this
> is not the case. The same rights are at stake in both places
> —the right to participate as citizens in a democratic society
> and to struggle against the same enemy. In Mississippi an
> autocratic and powerful minority rules, through organized
> violence, to suppress the vast, virtually powerless majority.
> In California, the privileged minority manipulates the Uni-
> versity bureaucracy to suppress the students' political ex-
> pression. That "respectable" bureaucracy masks the finan-
> cial plutocrats: that impersonal bureaucracy is the efficient
> enemy in a "Brave New World." In our free speech fight
> at the University of California, we have come up against
> what may emerge as the greatest problem of our nation—
> depersonalized, unresponsive bureaucracy.[26]

This is not the place to analyze more precisely the analo-
gies drawn between Mississippi and Berkeley. It is the old
demagogic device which always enhances the irrational feelings of a crowd. I would rather center our present discussion
around another point.

The university and bureaucracy, it has to be admitted,
resemble each other in a peculiar way. Both presuppose a
certain amount of existential restriction, or, if the term is per-
mitted, asceticism. The bureaucratic attitude restricted by
the impersonal limits of duties and responsibilities, and the
scientific attitude, restricted by the methodological limits of
science, require from man rationality and a certain suppres-
sion of emotions.

The modern mass university is easily pulled into society's
"functionalism" because it needs a strictly bureaucratic form
of organization. The traditional community model can no
longer be used in the modern university. It has to be organized bureaucratically. It is then only a small step to Kerr's

multiversity which sacrifices its independence to the functional demands of industrial society. Protests against this transformation are fully understandable, particularly in an emotional era like ours. However, rather than searching for the hazardous path between detachment and involvement, between theory and praxis, the Activist too easily gives way to his emotions and thereby barricades his road toward the future. He complains about frustration and alienation, but refuses to ask if an important part of this alienation does not stem from his own inability to cope with the rational forces of modern society. Theory and praxis are severed again, this time not by the ivory-tower bourgeois scientist, but by the Activist in favor of a self-proclaimed involvement, which he calls "praxis." It is, however, a praxis driven by the emotions of frustration. It rejects the generalizations of theory and refuses any form of compromise with institutional realities. Absolutism, based upon irrational violence, seems to be the only way out of this situation.

This protest, of course, reaches over the walls of the campus. It is actually directed toward society at large. In order to be more effective, Activism has been organized much more than Anarchism or Gnosticism. Organizations, such as the Student Non-violent Coordinating Committee (SNCC) or Students for a Democratic Society (SDS), are typically Activists' groups. Their structures are intentionally kept informal, non-bureaucratic and semi-anarchistic.[27]

Among the many groups and currents of the Activist type, usually collectively called the New Left, the SDS in particular has transcended the non-violent form of protest of the first half of the sixties. Many of its members profess the destruction of the existing order *without any clear alternatives*. As a result, protest is changed from means into goal. This then is another expression of contemporary absolutism. In the final analysis, Activists are as irrational and romantic as Gnosticists and Anarchists, the only difference being that their bravura in language and behavior entails graver implications. Having to legitimate themselves as genuine radicals by their very actions, Activists must rely more and more on the principle of violence. Romantic intellectuals, such as Herbert Marcuse and Jean-Paul Sartre, stand by and provide the Activist with

ideological justifications.[28] With an amazing naïveté as to
the implications of their philosophies, these Activist ideo-
logues call for and justify such ghastly principles as "intolerance" and "the barrel of the gun." They seem little disturbed
by the fact that the New Left neophytes adopt these principles with "few memories of the past, little definition of the
future" (Daniel Bell)[29] and an overdose of romanticism.
Sown in such soil, these principles easily grow into a new
kind of fascism. New Left philosophers are generally too certain about their own anti-fascism to be aware of the real
dangers of leftist fascism.

An important element in the philosophy of the New Left
is its repeated emphasis upon *direct or participatory democracy,* expressed in slogans like "Let the people decide themselves." This brings the New Left very near to populism,
which, if added to the recurrent complaint about alienation,
might result in fascist longings for a new community of plain
and common folks—a longing not foreign to American culture
anyway.[30]

Populism, as is well known, is narrowly related to the egali-
tarian and anti-intellectual mood of revivalism. It glorifies the
common rather than the uncommon and abhors the idea, as
Bell said, "that some are more qualified than others to assert
opinions." This anti-elitist mood, claims Bell, is tied to a special kind of social control: conduct is controlled through
"public" opinion rather than law. Law, of course, is essentially
traditional and immobile, often estranged from man's experiences and emotions, but therefore simultaneously free of
arbitrariness. The populist protest against law is typically
American. Says Bell:

> Americans . . . have often been impatient with law, and
> the quicker sanctions of vigilantism and shaming through
> opinion have predominated. Moreover, the small-town
> character of much of American temper derives its strength
> from the whispered play of gossip, from regulating conduct
> through public opinion.[31]

The New Left cry for direct democracy may easily acquire populist features. In the heat of the battle and the ex-

citement of the barricades, the Activist may well fail to see the congeniality of his emotional visions and the kind of populism preached by a category of Americans that is seemingly so remote from him, namely the common folks of the small-town community who believe in the American way and control their neighborhood by gossip, condemning those who are "different"—the Negro, the Jew, the Intellectual, and the Leftist Radical.

It was only a couple of decades ago that we saw in Germany what happens if society is remolded in accordance with the populist notion of a "healthy instinct of the people" (*gesundes Volksempfinden*). Indeed, the Nazis claimed to be the real democrats! It would be ridiculous to equate American populism or the Activist cry for participatory democracy with Nazism, but the combination of emotional hatred against an existing order and the longing for a new order in which man feels emotionally "at home" may well merge into a very dangerous and analogous force.[32]

Once again we witness how absolutism and extremism lead to a paradoxical coalescing of opposites. The Activist refuses to compromise with any form of authority and desires absolute democracy. But, as we saw before, absolute democracy is an impossibility since all absolutism involves one or another form of intolerance and violence. Incidentally, New Left absolutism also bears the other characteristic of all absolutism—the suicidal tendency. If all authority is rejected, it must also reject its own authorities. We then see the phenomenon of philosophers like Marcuse and Adorno, who applauded and assisted the course of the New Left, being attacked by their own followers. In short, absolutism admittedly is not the end of ideology, but it certainly is the end of democracy.

The Spirit of Protest and the Double Nature of Man

The spirit of protest arose among those who felt estranged from abstract society, its established power structure and economic affluence. It has, at the end of the sixties, reached the stage of violence, for which both the protesters and the forces of the Establishment are responsible. Barricades and burning streets are the witnesses of a growing revolt. There is, of course, an essential difference between the rioting poor in America's cities and the New Left students at Berkeley or Columbia, just as there was very little correspondence between the striking workers in France's industry in May 1968 and the students at the Sorbonne. The American poor and the French workers fight for economic and social equality, i.e. for a share in the existing affluence of modern society, whereas the militant students hate this very affluence and its corresponding middle-class life style. In other words, the workers want to share what the students try to overthrow. These two groups, the disadvantaged and the alienated, will never reach each other, even on the barricades. But the two of them do add to a revolutionary situation in which a very pervasive spirit of protest has been generated, penetrating deeply into contemporary socio-economic and political life. The three types of protest discussed in the present chapter manifest, in my opinion, a much more general dissatisfaction of modern man in an abstract society. They are expressions of a very fundamental malaise of democracy.

The three types of protest have in common a romantic aversion against institutional tradition: *the Activist* refuses to compromise with existing forms of institutional order and dreams of a totally new social order with absolute democracy. But apart from such generalities, he has no clear conception of a valid alternative to the present situation. *The Anarchist* dreams of total freedom in utopian visions where man is liberated from the restrictions of a traditional culture. *The Gnosticist* withdraws from society, to his inner world where he claims to find utter reality and final meaning.

Absolutism, we have seen time and again, is the most essential characteristic of the spirit of protest (cf. total freedom, utter reality, final meaning, absolute democracy, etc.) It is partly correct to view this absolutism and its corollary radicalism as essential elements of adolescence. The adolescent is haunted by unknown and still unco-ordinated emotions, by desires of a yet undefined nature, and by an awakening of a conscious awareness of realities that were taken for granted during his childhood. These emotions are vital and new; the institutions into which they have to be embedded, on the contrary, are old and traditional. Romantic *Sturm und Drang* is confronted by cold functionality and institutional tradition. There are, in addition to this, hardly any clear-cut ceremonial transitions left in modern secularized society, like the puberty rituals in primitive society (where the distance between childhood and adulthood is shorter anyhow). Such *rites de passage* indicate clearly the departure from one stage of life and the entrance into another: after the initiation of the puberty ritual has taken place, the primitive is an adult. In the absence of such clear-cut transitions, an emotional resistance may easily build up against the existing institutions of the "established" adult world—even to the point of rejection and violent revolt.

But, as I have said before, I do not believe that these facts about adolescence are sufficient to explain today's spirit of protest. Such an argument would simplify matters to the point of ridicule and may be left to the holders of power and their vested interests. As a matter of fact, one can assign quite another role to adolescence in contemporary society. By their very nature, adolescents are more aware of the fallacies and human dangers of abstract society than their socialized parents usually are. Not yet totally part of society's institutional life, the adolescent occupies a position favorable for relevant criticism. And many adults join their revolutionary ranks, in particular those who live at the outskirts of society by virtue of their social position, like artists and intellectuals. This, of course, is not to say that the spirit of protest has brought any valid solutions to the human problems of abstract society. All I claim here is that the critique of abstract society brought forward by many of the younger generation has some very relevant and valid elements.

Institutions do restrict individual freedom; they represent a traditional reality that offers a "sedimented" meaning system. Institutional limitation of freedom *can* assume inhuman qualities. Institutional reality can grow into a phantomlike superstructure detached from human experience. And it can hardly be denied that modern society has by and large become such a phantomlike, detached superstructure. But romantic absolutism cannot be an adequate remedy for man, because it leads to a coalescing of opposites. If driven to the extreme, freedom turns into oppression, love into hatred, reality into illusion, and meaning into absurdity. Man, in other words, needs the relativization of his own being. This relativization is offered by the traditional institutions.

Exteriority, man's dependence on an "alienating" outerworld of institutions, is a human condition. For the sake of communication, the human individual is compelled to leave the enclosures of his consciousness and inner life. He must direct his attention toward the others (cf. Feuerbach's "altruistic principle") and toward the institutions that direct and organize his behavior (cf. Plessner's "excentricity"). The individual is in danger of falling victim to manipulation if he fails to participate in this process of communication. He will be pushed around, not only by abstract institutions but by his own emotions as well. Man has to live in the balance of two poles, that of the individual realm with its unique physical constitution and personal consciousness, and that of his sociocultural environment with its traditional structures and its collective consciousness.

In sum, when man ceases to be a homo duplex and becomes either manipulated by an abstract society with alienating control or reduced to an anti-social individual by romantic absolutism, human existence is in a very hazardous situation. Both these situations occur in contemporary abstract society, as this and the former chapter have tried to demonstrate.

It is, in the final analysis, the principle of democracy that is at stake. Democracy as a form of society in which each individual receives the opportunity to realize his capacities to live a meaningful life, is possible only if man exists as homo duplex who has the power and the will to sacrifice his romantic longings for the rationality of institutional structures. He may lose the excitements of absolutism, but he will gain the possibility of expressing himself in a socially creative way. Homo duplex is neither rebel nor conformist, but moves between consensus and discontent. He therefore shares the uncertainties and tensions of democracy.

This completes our survey of forms of protest against abstract society. I want to stress once more that I have made no attempt to give a historical account of student unrest. For that, I refer to the appropriate literature.[33] The present discussion has to be viewed as a socio-philosophical interpretation which employs sociological observations and idealtypical generalizations.

Two specific issues demand deeper analysis. They came up time and again in the preceding discussion but did not receive full coverage. These issues are, first, institutional (or objective) autonomy vis-à-vis individual (or subjective) autonomy; and secondly, rationality vis-à-vis irrationality. Both problems result, as we will see in the next two chapters, from modern society's pluralism. They illustrate once more how the social ambiguity of man is torn apart in modern abstract society into two separated and often contradictory elements.

NOTES

1. For society as a model of communication, see C. Lévi-Strauss, *Structural Anthropology*, transl. by C. Jacobson, B. G. Schoepf (New York: Doubleday Anchor, 1967), pp. 208–303.
2. C. Wright Mills, *The Power Elite*, pp. 303 f. Cf. also his *Power, Politics and People* (New York: Ballantine Books, 1963), pp. 353–73.
3. C. Wright Mills, *The Power Elite*, p. 321. Such important elements of abstract society like opinion making and public relations cannot be discussed here. Cf. *Der Spiegel*, no. 28, July 8, 1968, p. 33: "Das Netz der Public Relations bleibt somit, wenn es fachmannisch geknuepft ist, fuer die Eingefangenen unsichtbar."
4. C. Wright Mills, *The Power Elite*, p. 320.
5. *Ibid.*, pp. 322 f.
6. *Ibid.*, p. 322.
7. David Riesman (with N. Glazer, R. Denney), *The Lonely Crowd* (New Haven: Yale University Press, 1966), p. 24.
8. *Ibid.*, p. 22.
9. *Ibid.*, p. 77.
10. Helmuth Schelsky, *Die Skeptische Generation* (Duesseldorf-Koeln: E. Diederichs Verlag, 1958), p. 491. This and other translations of quotations from Schelsky's book are mine (A.Z.).
11. *Ibid.*, p. 495.
12. *Ibid.*, p. 495.
13. *Newsweek*, December 18, 1967, p. 67: "Awaiting the Beatles is an eight-room block complete with marble bathtub, hot water, foam-rubber bedding, and air conditioning." Maharishi

Mahesh remarked: "Just as you have to water the roots of a tree, you have to water the mind through meditation."

14. Cf. the following remark by Timothy Leary: "Certain forms of sensory stimulation alter consciousness beyond games. The sexual orgasm is certainly the most frequent and natural, although so brief and so built into interpersonal courtship that it lost much of its mystical meaning in the West." In: D. Solomon, ed., *LSD: The Consciousness-Expanding Drug* (New York: Putnam, Berkeley Medallion Books, 1966), p. 110. Cf. also the following remark by a person who describes "the trip": "I have the suspicion that this whole business can, if one wants to play it that way, become a substitute for direct sexual activity, because there is an over-all increase in sensuousness. . . ." *Ibid.*, p. 94. It is, incidentally, typically gnostic to reject sexual intercourse because it depends on interpersonal courtship. As a matter of fact, masturbatory phantasies have always played an important role in Hellenistic gnostic cults.

15. Gilles Quispel, *Gnosis als Weltreligion* (Zuerich: Origo Verlag, 1952), p. 46: "Die wichtigste Gnosis unseres Jahrhunderts ist aber die komplexe Psychologie C. G. Jungs." For gnostic elements in Hegelianism and Marxism, see E. Topitsch, "Marxismus und Gnosis," in *Sozialphilosophie zwischen Ideologie und Wissenschaft* (Neuwied-Berlin: Luchterhand Verlag, 1961), pp. 235–71.

16. See Eric Voegelin, *Science, Politics and Gnosticism.*

17. Cf. Peter L. Berger, "Towards a Sociological Understanding of Psychoanalysis," in *Social Research* 32:1 (1965), 26–41.

18. D. Solomon, ed., "Preface," *o.c.*, p. viii.

19. *Ibid.*, p. 13.

20. The name Provo stems from an academic dissertation for a Ph.D. degree in social psychology. The author W. Buikhuizen (*Achtergronden van Nozemgedrag*, Assen 1965) gives an empirical analysis of the "skeptical" rather than "secessionist" generation. He applies the term "Provo" to a type of asocial youth who provokes for the sake of provocation as a kind of leisure activity. Secessionist Anarchists liked the word and adopted it as a name for their movement. See for a very good exposition of the development and aims of Provo: Roel van Duyn, *Het Witte Gevaar* (Amsterdam: Meulenhoff, 1967). Cf. also Hans Tuynman, *Full-Time Provo,* in Dutch (Amsterdam: De Bezige Bij, 1966). The following volume is a reader of articles on Provo and anarchism by various Dutch social scientists: F. E. Frenkel, ed., *Provo. Kanttekeningen bij een Deelverschijnsel* (Amsterdam: Van Gennep, 1967).

21. A kind of guerrilla situation arose: the police actions against these provocations made the Establishment unpopular among the Dutch population which initially did not sympathize with

the Provos at all. The Provos were, of course, fully aware of this and used it for their benefit.

22. Cf. my "Jokes and their Relation to Social Reality," in *Social Research* 35:2 (1968), 286–312.

23. Arnold Gehlen coined the appropriate term "intellectual trapeze."

24. C. Kerr, *The Uses of the University* (Cambridge, Mass.: Harvard University Press, 1963). Cf. also Richard Lichtman, "The University: Mask for Privilege?" in *The Center Magazine* (The Center for the Study of Democratic Institutions), 1:2 (January 1968), 2–10, and Kerr's reply, *ibid.*, pp. 13 f.

25. M. Cohen, D. Hale, eds., *The New Student Left* (Boston: Beacon Press, 1967), p. 236. Cf. for a more generalized analysis of the New Left: J. Newfield, *A Prophetic Minority* (New York: A Signet Book, 1967). See also in this context George F. Kennan, *Democracy and the Student Left* (New York: Bantam Books, 1968).

26. M. Cohen, D. Hale, eds., *o.c.*, p. 249.

27. Cf. H. Zinn, *SNCC: The New Abolitionists* (Boston: Beacon Press, 1965).

28. See for Sartre's view on violence his preface to Frantz Fanon's *The Wretched of the Earth* (New York: Grove Press, 1966). Marcuse's opinions on this subject can be found in *A Critique of Pure Tolerance*, a volume of essays by R. P. Wolff, B. Moore, Jr., and H. Marcuse (Boston: Beacon Press, 1966). Cf. for critique of Marcuse, M. Cranston, "Herbert Marcuse," in *Encounter*, March 1969, pp. 38–50. See also Hannah Arendt, "Reflections on Violence," in *The New York Review of Books*, February 27, 1969, pp. 19–31. In Germany, professors J. Habermas and T. Adorno of the so-called Frankfurt School have played the role of New Left philosophers. Ironically but understandably, their increasingly radicalized students have now turned against them. See Jochen Steinmayr, "The Revolution Is Devouring Its Parents," in *Encounter*, May 1969, pp. 30 f.

29. Daniel Bell, *The End of Ideology*, 1960 (New York: Collier Books, 1961), p. 397.

30. To relate the notion of "participatory (or direct) democracy" to populism was suggested by G. van Benthem van den Bergh, "Studenten en Politiek in de Verenigde Staten: de New Left," in F. E. Frenkel, *o.c.*, pp. 51–73.

31. D. Bell, *o.c.*, p. 115.

32. Add to this populism the obvious delight in protest and revolt, and we are at a kind of *vivere pericolosamente* as professed by the Italian fascists. *Der Spiegel*, no. 29, July 15, 1968, p. 28, reports in its coverage of the Paris "revolution" in 1968 that activist students in Berlin and Paris now call themselves "left fascists." This, it seems to me, is a significant fact. The same weekly (no. 25, June 17, 1968, pp. 84 ff.) gives also a report

on the actions of France's special police force, the CRS (Compagnies républicaines de sécurité) against the students. Reading this report, which is based on material from eye witnesses, one is compelled to draw comparisons with the actions of Nazi Germany's special force, the SS. See for an English survey of the student revolt at German universities: "The Cult of Violence. A Special Report from Germany," in *Encounter*, May 1969, pp. 26–35. This report was prepared by the editors and correspondents of *Der Spiegel*.

33. See for an extensive bibliography: P. G. Altbach, *Student Politics and Higher Education in the United States: A Select Bibliography* (published by United Ministries in Higher Education, St. Louis, Mo. and the Center for International Affairs, Harvard University, Cambridge, Mass., 1968). This volume carries an enlightening introduction by Seymour M. Lipset, "American Student Activism," pp. 1–14.

5

AUTONOMY
IN PLURALISTIC SOCIETY

Introduction

As a young man, Hegel supported the cause of the French Revolution. Together with many intellectuals and artists of his day, he greeted this turning point in the course of European civilization as the fundamental liberation of man. They were all intoxicated by a new sense of freedom. Very soon, however, Hegel was plagued by feelings of fear and doubt—gradually at first, but increasingly strongly after the terror of the Robespierre regime had begun. The freedom of the revolution, Hegel discovered, had created a void which was now filled up with the cruelest forms of Jacobinian subjection and tyranny. Instead of creating room for humanism, the revolution had brought political repression and dehumanization of the worst kind. Reactionary forces took their chance, and this trend continued throughout the nineteenth century. Realizing this, Hegel was haunted by the ambiguity of freedom, namely its promise and its terror. He tried to reconcile the paradox in his later philosophical system.[1]

Whatever value one attributes to Hegel's philosophy today, one can hardly deny that the paradoxical experience of freedom as simultaneously promise and terror has characterized Western man and his philosophy until this very day. In industrial and pluralistic society, the promise and terror of freedom have acquired an additional dimension which was absent in Hegel's time. The freedom of the modern individual is continuously limited by various forms of coercion and social control stemming from different institutional sectors. The novelty of modern social control lies in the fact that the individual is controlled by many, often independent institutional patterns, while he is hardly able to grasp this control existentially and intellectually because of the structural complexity of pluralistic society. Thus to the modern individual pluralistic society is no longer a coherent meaningful universe, and its control is experienced as an alienating and dehumanizing force. Another aspect must be added to this.

Contemporary society exhibits a disparity between the individual and the institutional structures of his society. The latter have the tendency to grow independent and to exist for their own sake. The individual, on the other hand, seems to take the opposite road, to withdraw from the public sphere into his private world and grow increasingly autonomous, often in a rather subjectivistic way. As Thomas Luckmann has formulated it, modern society shows a *discrepancy between the subjective autonomy of the individual and the objective autonomy of the social institutions.*[2] In this situation, the individual experiences a very pervasive social control (which he calls "alienation"), but also a great amount of private autonomy (which he calls "freedom").

I shall focus the present chapter on a socio-philosophical interpretation of this paradoxical experience of control and "alienation" on the one hand, and private autonomy and "freedom" on the other. This experience is related to a structural paradox: *being pluralistic, modern society controls the individual in many different ways. This control is strong, but never total.* The individual, that is, is controlled by partial allegiances to different groups and by a power structure in which he is partly dominated, partly dominant. In other words, there is in pluralistic society no coherence and uniformity of domination and control. As a result, the social structure leaves voids which the individual fills up with private autonomy, that is with his dreams, fantasies, desires and utopias. This gives him the feeling of freedom and independence. It is experienced as a private, unalienable and rather emotional phenomenon. No wonder that the rebellion against pluralistic society arose by and large from this private and basically irrational autonomy of the individual. The voids of the social structure at large are believed to be the "realm of freedom," untouched yet by the alienation of institutional control.

The present chapter will discuss these points in more detail, starting with an analysis of the nature of control and coercion in modern society. The paradox of the objective autonomy of social institutions vis-à-vis the subjective autonomy of the modern individual is explained with the help of the concept of pluralistic society. Finally, the modern experience of "freedom" as escape from social control is viewed and assessed as an illusion stemming from a fundamental lack of insight into the nature of modern man's autonomy.

One final introductory remark: these issues are seen as structural problems, but looked at from the point of view of the individual who is affected by them. In other words, I pretend that the problems under discussion are not sociological constructions but elements of the "natural world" of the individual in modern society.

Coercion in Pluralistic Society

Modern man often complains in various voices about social control and views himself as the victim of unidentifiable powers. The professional who worries about his taxes, the cab driver who philosophizes about "those guys in city hall," the SDS student who protests against "the system," all share the same feeling of powerlessness. The catchword for this experience is "alienation." The proposed remedies and solutions differ widely, but are all born of a longing for some kind of power. As I have said, I interpret this experience as a consequence of the particular structural situation of modern society.

The structural peculiarity of industrial society compared to pre-industrial societies lies in its pluralism. The concept of *pluralistic society*, we saw before, stands for the notion that industrial society is made up of various institutionally isolated sectors which require from the modern individual the ability to play disparate roles, thus imprinting on him disparate identities. In pre-industrial society, these sectors (the family, religion, formal education, army, government, etc.)

were still functionally and culturally interwoven and inter-
dependent. Today, they have grown more and more apart
(cf. Dahrendorf's theory of institutional isolation, discussed in
the third chapter). The sectors of modern society are, of
course, still functionally related to each other, but they fail
to provide the individual with one coherent system of meaning. He has to change meanings continuously while moving
from one sector to the other. And even within these sectors
he belongs to different groups and groupings which require
a multitude of allegiances. Since such groups are more often
than not short-term associations that dissolve after their goal
has been realized, and since no individual is able to adhere
with his total personality to several groups at once, the individual's allegiance to his groups is necessarily of a partial and
rather detached nature. This has grave implications for human interrelations. Friendships, for example, become increasingly superficial. But it also has, in a wider sense, implications
for the relationship of the individual to his institutional environment. Having only partial allegiance to various groups to
which he belongs, while changing roles like the jackets of a
wardrobe, the modern individual can no longer maintain the
bond between himself and the institutions of his society. In
short, a distance has grown between the individual and modern society. Pre-industrial man was still an indissoluble part
of his social totality (the totemic clan, the Greek polis, the
medieval Corpus Christianum) and his world view had no
room for separations of subject and object, individual and
society, freedom and control.[3] His socio-cultural reality was
experienced as a micro-cosmos—ordered, closed, stable and
uniform. Pluralistic society, on the contrary, is an "open"
society, not determined by a traditional and sacred past but
pushed forward in a continuous movement of development
and change to which we have given the pretentious name
"progress."

In such a pluralistic context, the problem of freedom and
control acquires some peculiar structural dimensions. Sociologically speaking, coercion and control are the corollaries of
certain established *power and authority relations.* Following
Max Weber, one can define power as the chance one has to
carry one's will through over against the will of others; and

authority as the chance that a command will be obeyed by a specific group of people. Dahrendorf adds:

> The important difference between power and authority consists in the fact that whereas power is essentially tied to the personality of individuals, authority is always associated with social positions. . . . It is only another way of putting this difference if we say—as does Max Weber—that while power is merely a factual relation, authority is a legitimate relation of domination and subjection. In this sense, authority can be described as legitimate power.[4]

Power and authority thus presuppose a relationship of domination and subjection, or as Simmel put it, of superordination and subordination.

Marx, as is well known, viewed this relationship in macrosociological terms as two opposing classes which were bound to clash in a revolution. In this scheme, domination is represented by the capitalist bourgeois class, and subordination by the proletariat. These classes are not so much strata in the sense of social stratification as reciprocal conflicting groups. But, as Dahrendorf has demonstrated, Marx's picture of domination and subordination in terms of two monolithic conflicting groups is much too simple to be true for industrial society. Conflicting groups, he claims, are rather loose aggregations in modern society: they arise for the sake of certain interests within the setting of particular associations.[5]

Dahrendorf then defines classes as groups that strive for the realization of their interests. They are, consequently, power and conflict groups. In some situations, a particular conflict group may hold power and thus be dominant, in others the same group may be devoid of power and thus subordinate. Domination and subjection are, therefore, distributed over a pluralistic scale of power and authority. Theoretically speaking, an individual can be equally dominant and subordinated, depending on the configuration of the groups to which he belongs. In reality, however, Dahrendorf asserts, a sort of superimposition will occur. The powerful meet recurrently in different associations, and so do the subjected. A formation of blocs is apt to develop along the demarcation lines that separate domination from subordination. But such a superimposition will never lead to the macrosociological uniformity of Marx's model of two conflicting classes. The coercive forces of power and authority in modern society remain distributed over a pluralistic scale and rarely petrify into clearly identifiable structures with clearly identifiable repression mechanisms.[6]

Dahrendorf's pluralistic model of power and authority structures is relevant to our interpretation of modern man's experience of pervasive yet ephemeral control. Apart from possible superimposition (which, incidentally, Dahrendorf never really specifies), coercive power hardly ever occurs in concrete formations of antagonistic classes. The individual in pluralistic society knows that he is coerced and controlled, but he knows this as an individual, not as a class member. He is coerced within his specific configuration of associations and groups, and he shares this particular configuration with a handful of others who are part of his "private life." In addition, the pressures he has to endure are counterbalanced by the dominating power he himself may hold in certain other social positions. In such a situation, class consciousness can never emerge. Every New Left activist knows how much the pluralistic scale of power and authority impedes the realization of his goals: it is hard to create class consciousness since the dominated in society are only partially dominated and tend to retreat to the private sphere where they can escape the pressures of society. The Blacks in North America are perhaps the only potential proletariat with possible class consciousness—those Blacks, that is, who are not yet part of the black bourgeoisie. For the rest, all attempts to instigate a revolution in our leveled society (Helmuth Schelsky) are doomed to remain abortive.

A further observation can now be added. In his famous essay on superordination and subordination, Georg Simmel pointed out that an individual is never subjected to power with his *total* personality.[7] That is, one is never totally involved in the social relationship of superordination and subordination. This, Simmel claims, is typical of all social relations. One is, for instance, never married with all of one's personality, one is never completely citizen, member of a religious congregation, soldier in the army, etc.[8] Because of this partial adherence to roles on the part of his subjects, a ruler can exert his powerful domination rather easily and successfully. This is particularly true of crowds. In a crowd, Simmel asserts, the individual is only superficially involved. It is not his total personality that is at stake. Therefore, he is more willing to submit to power and domination than he would be in cases where a total involvement would be required of him. Revolt always occurs when individuals are no longer allowed to develop some kind of private spontaneity and freedom. We may draw from this the following conclusion: *coercion and control are more successful and more severe in groups (or societies) that require only partial involvement than they are in groups (or societies) that demand total involvement and total obedience.* In other words, control defeats its purpose when it becomes totalitarian. It will be strong and severe if it coerces the individual only partially and leaves room for some privacy.

Simmel's observation is, of course, of great value to our present discussion. It explains the seeming paradox of pervasive control and increased private autonomy: *social control in pluralistic society is so strong and pervasive precisely because of the privatization of the modern individual.* This privatization, or subjective autonomy, can be explained as the result of the increased segmentation of industrial society.

Coercion and Bureaucracy

Everyday complaints about coercion in modern society often focus on bureaucracy—its unresponsiveness, its rigmarole, its dehumanizing tendency. Many of our jokes expose these features and simultaneously express our irritations with them. Bureaucracy reduces one's personality to a calculable factor, a number, a punch card, part of the filing system. It must do so in order to function properly. Daily experiences like these may not, of course, serve as sociological explanations but they are important indications of certain trends and developments in modern social life. No social scientist may alienate himself from these experiences of the individual in his "natural world." The complaints about coercive bureaucracy, therefore, demand our attention.

Pre-industrial society, as we saw in the second chapter, may be viewed as a coherent cosmos or meaningful universe held together by sacred traditions. There is a strong and continuous awareness that the ancestors made this life in the here-and-now possible. Regressing into the sacred past, the individual encounters the gods who created this world "at the beginning," *bereshith, in illo tempore.* The present is merely a repetition of the primeval time "at the beginning" when the original event of creation took place. This time and this event are commemorated in myths and rituals.[9] Thus the world is kept together by religion—not in the form of canonized doctrines and beliefs but in countless rituals and a whole style of life. Religion is not one element of primitive life—it is life itself. Religion is not an institutional part of the primitive social structure, the social structure itself is religious.[10]

Industrial society is a segmented and highly differentiated society with several independent institutional sectors that have the tendency to grow into autonomous "sub-societies." Being father, member of the tribal council and warrior are, in primitive society, interrelated parts of one single identity; and they are seen as the corollaries of one religious responsibility. Being father, professional in one or another organization and soldier in the nation's army, are, to the individual in modern society, three totally different roles with three different identities, based upon different responsibilities. Religion no longer binds together the different sectors of life; it has been institutionally isolated into one sector among many, and in the process, it has been relativized into merely one possible explanation of life and the world. This is generally called secularization.[11] In the consciousness of modern man, religion is largely restricted to a particular institutional sector (the Church) where it functions as a kind of private preference on the part of individuals. Recently, forms of religiosity have been emerging outside institutionalized religion (cf. the religiosity of hippies, the interest in witchcraft, magic and astrology),[12] but they have not as yet penetrated into the larger structures of society. By and large, religion has lost its integrating function with regard to society as a whole.

However, industrial society is obviously not an anarchistic chaos. It is apparently still held together in one way or the other. One can then raise the legitimate question as to *which force in pluralistic society has taken over from religion its integrative function.* Religion has always been the main force of social integration while playing a very strong coercive role. Its substitute in modern society must also exhibit these integrative and coercive features. Taking certain ideas in Weber's discussion of rational organization to their extreme, I propose to *view modern bureaucracy as the general coercive force in pluralistic society that keeps this society together as a functionally integrated whole.*

There is no need to discuss bureaucracy in detail at this point, but merely to draw attention to some of its main characteristics. The first aspect that calls for our attention is its formalism. Bureaucracy is a form of organization (or better, a form of organizing) that can be applied to substantially different institutions and organizations. The Church as well as the hospital, the army as well as the university apply bureaucratic principles of organization. Bureaucracy has spread out over all the sectors of industrial society. It can be found in economic, political, religious, educational and artistic organizations.[13] To whatever sector the individual turns these days, he encounters bureaucracy with its uniform features of files, memos and the impersonal bureaucratic attitude. There are some unimportant differences of style: the bureaucrat in city hall may lack the uncommitted smile of the bank employee, but everyone knows that the kindness of the latter is imposed upon him for the sake of public rather than personal relations. Bureaucracy, as Weber said, is based upon functional expertise and requires impersonal, detached attitudes. It works "without regard for persons" and *sine ira ac studio*—in cold blood. Bureaucrats who perform their role appropriately do not hate, nor do they love; they do their job. Weber has related this correctly to the increasing segmentation of modern society:

The more complicated and specialized modern culture becomes, the more its external supporting apparatus demands the personally detached and strictly "objective" *expert,* in lieu of the master of older social structures, who was moved by personal sympathy and favor, by grace and gratitude. Bureaucracy offers the attitudes demanded by the external apparatus of modern culture in the most favorable combination.[14]

Office hierarchy is an essential element of bureaucracy. It creates "a firmly ordered system of super- and subordination in which there is a supervision of the lower offices by the higher ones" (Weber). Bureaucracy not only, like religion, integrates society-at-large in a functional way, it also creates, again like religion, systems of domination and subordination throughout all of society. In addition to this, we must bear in mind that all modern individuals have been socialized into the bureaucratic attitude. Indeed, this attitude has spilled over from bureaucracy proper to social life in general. Being frustrated by bureaucrats, we hate the official rather than the person who does his job. Socialized into the bureaucratic attitude, we are coerced by bureaucracy far beyond its proper "jurisdiction"—it has penetrated deeply into our consciousness and personality. In this respect too, bureaucracy resembles religion!

But there is, of course, a very crucial difference between religion in pre-industrial and bureaucracy in industrial society. Prior to the process of industrialization, religion was still able to provide the individual with coherent meaning, to bind society together into a meaningful universe which gave man certainty and stability, and, most important of all: an ascribed, meaningful identity. Its integrative force was not merely functional: it bound the individual to a sacred past of ancestors and gods, it gave him a place among his fellow men, and it guaranteed him a relatively predictable future. see p 72 In short, religion tied the individual to the "social facts" (Durkheim) of his society which, not amazingly, were experienced as religious facts. Bureaucracy can never assume this function! It is just a formalistic principle of organization that does not, and cannot, care about a meaningful existence for the individual. Its main interest is efficiency, and its integration is of a purely functional nature. Bureaucracy is only "meaningful" in view of its organizational goals. To the total life experience of the individual, this same bureaucracy often appears as utterly senseless and meaningless. This is once more an indication of the discrepancy between the objective autonomy of institutional structures (to which bureaucracy has contributed so much) and the subjective autonomy of the individual in pluralistic society.

The Experience of Freedom

The objective autonomy of the social institutions (or institutional sectors) of pluralistic society helps to explain the pervasive yet ephemeral control the individual experiences. We must now focus upon the modern individual's subjective autonomy.

As was said, the individual is no longer able to relate to his social environment as a total personality. His partial allegiances to various groups and groupings have led to an increasing distance between him and the institutional structures. As the objective structures grow more and more abstract and lose their meaning contents, the individual withdraws more and more into the private sphere. Luckmann made the segmentation of society into more or less independent sectors responsible for this process of privatization:

Personal identity becomes, essentially, a private phenomenon. This is, perhaps, the most revolutionary trait of modern society. Institutional segmentation left wide areas in the life of the individual unstructured and the overarching biographical context of significance undetermined. From the interstices of the social structure that resulted from institutional segmentation emerged what may be called a "private sphere." The "liberation" of individual consciousness from the social structure and the "freedom" in the "private sphere" provide the basis for the somewhat illusory sense of autonomy which characterizes the typical person in modern society.[15]

Pluralistic society is no longer the coherent, meaningful universe it had been before. Because of segmentation, the social structure of modern society leaves voids (Luckmann: interstices) which the individual fills up with his private meanings, his dreams, phantasies, explanations and justifications. Since they lie between the institutional segments of pluralistic society, these private meanings escape the control and rationality of the rest of the social structure and are experienced as the subjective and unalienable foundation of human existence. The individual calls this his private autonomy, or even "freedom," but is unaware of the fact that this "freedom" is merely *residual:* it is, so to speak, put together from the leftovers of a segmented social structure. These leftovers are embellished with uncommitted feelings, sentiments and irrationalities. The intellectual style is made up of free-floating impressions. With Luckmann, one might call this "freedom" largely illusory.

At this point, the reader may well have some serious objections. Up to now, he may claim, we have contrasted segmented modern society with the relatively homogeneous structures of pre-industrial societies. Granted that man in pre-modern society experiences a concrete meaning and reality, does he have any freedom? Is he not completely enslaved by a predetermined social position? What are the opportunities for him to transcend the social limits set up around him from birth? Are not the Greek *polis*, the medieval estates, the tyrannically organized Asian societies and the primitive tribes of Africa and South America, forms of *societal totalitarianism?* Is not, in contrast to this, pluralistic society the best guarantee for genuine human freedom?

We are confronted here, in my opinion, with one of the most tenacious prejudices of Western civilization. It is the notion that man in the Common Human Pattern is still enslaved by his socio-cultural environment, whereas modernization has brought mankind liberation from social bondage and genuine freedom. But what precisely is this genuine freedom? Under closer scrutiny it appears to be very individualistic: it is *my* individual freedom that *I* have to realize in *my* life. Existence is the very realization of this freedom. Indeed, existentialism is the best-known ideology of this individualistic concept of freedom. As Sartre himself realized in his *Critique de la Raison Dialectique* (1960), existentialism presents a typically bourgeois philosophy which places man outside his social context while putting all the emphasis on his individual existence.[16]

This existentialist conception of freedom has penetrated very deeply into modern consciousness. Today, we can hardly conceive of freedom as an element of man's *social* existence. We tend to see it almost exclusively in psychological terms as part of our *individual* and *private* existence. Since Luther, freedom has been reserved exclusively for *homo internus.*

Now, we naturally miss the point completely if we apply this individualistic concept of freedom to the relatively closed and homogeneous societies of the Common Human Pattern. The awareness of being an inseparable part of the social collectivity is so strongly rooted in the consciousness of premodern man that individual freedom in private seclusion falls outside any range of possibilities. This does not, however, imply that pre-industrial society lacks any form of freedom. The question is rather what freedom means in the frame of reference of the Common Human Pattern.

To begin with, one must realize that freedom does not pose any serious problems to pre-modern man. Of course, there were philosophers who brooded over man's free will, but they never reached the verge of anxiety and despair so typical of modern existentialists, precisely because of their firm trust in the Logos, Jahwe or God. For example, if one compares the scholastic debates about the free will with the existentialist anxiety as to human freedom and individual responsibility, one can hardly escape the impression that these medieval theologians were playing with concepts rather than struggling with existential problems. To them, freedom was not really much of a problem. It was real by being absent as a problem.

It is important, at this point, to remind the reader of the intrinsic relationship between meaning, reality and freedom. If life is experienced as concrete and meaningful, freedom will be part of it by being absent as a problem. He is free who experiences social reality as meaningful and who knows his position and identity as traditional and taken-for-granted qualities. The moment doubt is cast upon this meaning and reality, freedom becomes a problem. When the structures become "alien," alienation poses itself as an existential problem. Freedom then becomes something to search for, a goal to obtain, a value to realize. The anthropological field worker will encounter considerable problems in explaining the concept of freedom, as we know it, to a member of a totemistic clan, whereas the nineteenth-century proletariat in the slums of industrial cities understood Marx's theory of human freedom perfectly well!

In sum, freedom is existentially real if it is absent as a problem; it will be existentially absent if it is real as a problem. In other words, there is no objective definition of freedom that can be applied universally to all societies, because freedom depends on the experience of meaning and reality in a given social frame of reference. Pluralistic society is an abstract society with an atrophied experience of meaning and reality. Such a society might, admittedly, leave much room for individual choices, but it is questionable if such liberty constitutes human freedom. The increasing discrepancy between objective and subjective autonomy does certainly not warrant such a conclusion.

Conclusion

Industrial society has a segmented and differentiated social structure. It is, in the experience of the modern individual, an abstract society that does not fulfill his desire for meaning, reality and freedom. These he claims to find within the perimeters of his private and subjectivistic existence. The autonomy of societal structures is a crucial aspect of modern life. The structures (or institutional sectors, as we have also called them) are to a large extent not only mutually isolated but also independent of the individual. In other words, modern man faces his society as a relatively autonomous reality to which he experiences but little correspondence. This gap between the individual and his institutional environment is enlarged still further by his tendency to withdraw into his private autonomy where he claims to experience freedom.

Parallel to this problem of coercion and freedom, runs the discrepancy between rationality and irrationality in modern abstract society. Here again, we observe the fundamental paradox of contemporary man vis-à-vis an abstract society.

NOTES

1. See for an excellent discussion of Hegel's early philosophy: H. Schmidt, *Verheissung und Schrecken der Freiheit* (Stuttgart: Kreuz Verlag, 1964). This book presents a philosophical and theological discussion of the notion of freedom in existentialism against the background of Hegel's early philosophical thought. Cf. also J. Ritter, *Hegel und die Franzoesische Revolution* (Koeln-Opladen, 1957) which I had not yet the chance to read.

2. Thomas Luckmann, *The Invisible Religion* (New York: Macmillan, 1967). This intriguing discussion of the individual in pluralistic society has greatly influenced my thoughts on this issue. I should also mention here Peter L. Berger and Thomas Luckmann, *The Social Construction of Reality* (New York: Doubleday Anchor, 1966).

3. We return to this important point at the end of this chapter.

4. Ralf Dahrendorf, *Class and Class Conflict in Industrial Society,* 1959 (London: Routledge & Kegan Paul, 1963), p. 166.

5. *Ibid.,* p. 202.

6. This, of course, was the main critique against C. Wright Mills's notion of a power elite ruling contemporary American society in a more or less monolithic way.

7. Georg Simmel, *Soziologie* (Berlin: Duncker & Humblot, 1958), pp. 115–17.

8. This is similar to Mead's notion of the "I" and the "Me" in the "Social Self." The "me," as we saw in the second chapter, consists of internalized roles and is only part of the self or personality.

9. These points were made in several studies of Mircea Eliade. See in particular his *Cosmos and History.*

10. These formulations follow Durkheim. See for a recent adaptation of Durkheim's approach in these matters, Thomas Luckmann, *o.c.*

11. The relation between pluralism and secularization has been clearly elaborated by Peter L. Berger, *The Sacred Canopy* (New York: Doubleday Anchor, 1967).

12. For a good discussion of these issues, see A. M. Greeley, *Religion In The Year 2000* (New York: Sheed & Ward, 1969).

13. The only sector still exempt from bureaucracy's influences is the family. (It is consequently the main niche for privatization.) Its relations to society at large, however, are very much

bureaucratized (cf. family allowance, insurance, medical care, etc.).

14. Max Weber, *From Max Weber: Essays in Sociology*, eds. H. Gerth, C. W. Mills (New York: Oxford University Press, 1958), p. 216.
15. Thomas Luckmann, *o.c.*, p. 97.
16. Cf. Jean-Paul Sartre, *In Search for a Method*, transl. by H. Barnes (New York: Knopf, 1963). A good summary of Sartre's *Critique de la Raison Dialectique* is given by W. Desan, *The Marxism of Jean-Paul Sartre* (New York: Doubleday Anchor, 1965).

6

RATIONALITY
AND IRRATIONALITY[1]

Introduction

Since Max Weber it has been common sociological knowledge that the increased segmentation and bureaucratization of industrial society causes a growing rationalization.[2] The present chapter is concerned with the paradox that, despite the increased rationalization of modern society, the human experience has grown irrational. Facing a social world which is, as we have seen, detached from human experience, many a modern man has been thrown back upon his own subjectivity and lives his life emotionally and often irrationally. Modern subjectivism is largely irrational because it is not channeled by the rationality of institutions, is indeed an escape from the institutions of a strange and abstract society. That means, despite the growing rationalization of industrial and bureaucratic society, modern man has become increasingly irrational. In his search for meaning, reality and freedom, he relies not on traditional institutions, but on subjective emotions.

To tackle the main problems involved in this paradox of rationality and irrationality we must consider the relationship between institutions and emotions. A sound sociological theory of emotions does not exist as yet, but we can lay down the basic principles. It is important to remember first of all that human emotions are not only channeled by institutions but also receive a great deal of stimulation from them. Man therefore loses an important source of stimulation when he turns away from his institutions! But before we discuss these matters, some methodological questions have to be raised.

Methodological Assumptions

A sociological analysis of emotions relates experiences like love, fear, joy and hatred to institutional structures without engaging in a lengthy discussion of their psychological and physiological aspects, just as the classic sociology of knowledge did not engage specifically in physiological or psychological debates on cognition. But in order not to confuse things by vague concepts, some categories have to be cleared up first.

I use the concept "emotions" to stand for the *common-sense notion* of love, fear, anger, faith, joy, hatred, etc. etc. And it is the common-sense everyday experience that I will try to interpret. In other words, I will avoid the models of psychology and physiology. The "emotions" covered by these scientific models are not necessarily identical with the emotions experienced by man in his everyday life. The "emotions" analysed by psychology and physiology are, at base, pre-defined components of constructed models ruled by the constructed laws of cause and effect. For the sociologist, it is important to remember that emotions may fit in a stimulus-response effect, but they are in reality very rarely part of a rational process of cause and effect. On the contrary, emotions are the most unpredictable aspects of human life and often merge in unintelligible combinations. As a result, authors like Dostoyevsky have generally been more successful in describing man's emotional life than the best physiologists or psychologists. A scientific analysis of emotions, conditioned by the laws of causality, can only reduce emotional life to certain pre-conceived and pre-constructed models. These models are meant as heuristic devices for the clarification of human emotions, but they are, as such, unable to give a comprehensive picture of what emotions are and what they mean to the individual in everyday life. They are not meant to be comprehensive, a feature that they share with all scientific models, and are useful only in the frame of reference of particular scientific interests.

This is not to say that the sociologist does not use models.

He is certainly not a Dostoyevsky. But, without asking for a scientific explanation of the very nature of emotions (e.g. their physiological and psychological constitution), the sociologist relates the non-scientific, naïve experience of emotions to its societal frame of reference.[3]

The psychologist and physiologist who want to know the precise nature and the origin of emotions may, of course, not rely on naïve everyday experiences of emotions. But for the sociologist who tries to interpret the relationship between emotions and institutions, it suffices to know that emotions occur and that common sense calls them fear, hatred, love, anger, etc. He analyzes what total man experiences, not what the scientific models indicate. In these models, "emotions" are subjected to the laws of cause and effect and ruled by rationality—the rationality by which the models have been constructed. In everyday life, on the contrary, emotions often escape man's rational capacities, yielding irrational actions and emotional thoughts. The sociologist is particularly interested in this irrationality, which he confronts with the functional rationality of social institutions. The disparity between emotions and institutions leads to some interesting sociological observations, which are naturally placed in the frame of reference of a rational model, the sociological model. But this *logical rationality* does not necessarily affect the irrationality of everyday emotions and the rationality of social institutions. In other words, one should distinguish between the logical rationality of scientific models and the existential rationality and irrationality of everyday life where even the highest degree of rationality is mixed with irrationality.[4]

I define rationality as the search for means believed to be adequate for the realization of clearly envisaged goals. According to this definition, rain magic is as rational as scientifically designed irrigation systems since it is believed (in an act of thought) to be an adequate means for the inundation of the fields—just as we moderns believe the jet plane to be an adequate means for reaching a certain destination fast and safely. It is this belief that makes behavior rational. Instead of calling magic "irrational," we might interpret our steady belief in a technology we hardly understand to be essentially of a magical nature. In addition to this, one should bear in mind that rational behavior is largely predictable and calculable because of this very sequence of means and goals.

Emotions are irrational in that they pay little attention to adequate means and clearly defined goals. They are therefore often neither predictable nor calculable. Being insulted, one experiences an emotional rage which seeks an outlet. Of course, one may decide to control oneself and react rationally by taking one's time to search for the best way to take revenge. But if one gets "carried away" and tries to relieve one's rage by slamming doors or running amok, one's behavior can be called irrational.[5]

Calling emotions irrational, the sociologist hints at the behavioral aspect of emotions. However, not all emotional behavior is necessarily irrational. A person overcome by fury may decide, as I have said, to remain "rational." This rationality, however, is clearly imposed on the original emotion and not an inherent aspect of it. The rationality is imposed on the emotion of fury by institutions! This leads to a further consideration.

Human rationality is not just the product of individual acts of thought and reflection. If an insulted individual decides to control his rage and remain rational, he is able to do so only because he has been socialized in a world of institutions that control him. The institutions with their traditional norms and values provide the individual with the models of rationality. Institutions are established and traditional patterns of behavior which have their origins in the division of labor. As such, they display the functional rationality of the principle of efficiency. Lacking an internal organization of instincts and their "genetic logic," human behavior is rational only because of institutional control. This leads us to assert that man will become ever more irrational if the institutions of his society fail to keep him under their control.

Emotions are not kept under rational control exclusively. They may also rationalize themselves into symbolic systems. Rationalized emotions are usually called ideologies. An ideology is a rational defense of certain interests that are based on emotionally and irrationally adhered to positions. Asked for his logical rationale, the ideologist, pressed hard enough, can only point at some emotionally held "convictions," "beliefs," or "dreams."

This point is quite important, since ideologies are often institutionally disguised, functioning as semi-rational but fundamentally irrational legitimations of the actions undertaken by certain interest groups. Institutions are, as was said above, models of rationality, but they often hide an ideological and thus irrational content. For that reason, an age of institutional crisis in which man turns inward to his irrational subjectivity has to be an age of flourishing ideologies. Even if modern man is estranged from his institutions and considers them as alienating structures, he may still follow their ideological content because of their irrational and emotional nature. In such a situation, the institution marriage loses its traditional stature, but the ideology of romantic love is stronger than ever before; the institution church is pushed to the periphery of modern consciousness, but the individual is emotionally religious in every fiber of his existence; the modern state is considered to be an alienating Leviathan, but we are more political in our attitudes and thoughts today than ever before.[6]

Institutions and Emotions

A sociological theory of institutions begins with an account of the anthropological nature of institutions.[7]

Human emotions lack the major biological channels and stimuli that characterize the emotions of animals. Endowed with but a few instincts (that is, instinctive residues rather than fully developed instincts), the human being has to find the directives and incentives for his behavior and his emotions elsewhere, namely outside himself in a cultural environment of institutions.

This is not to say that the origin of emotions is not biological, but rather that the instinctual equipment for the display of emotions is lacking in the human being. The expression of emotions is culturally learned, and after it has been learned biological consequences occur. For instance, I learn to be afraid of a man with a knife. Once learned, this emotional reaction will be automatic (i.e. semi-instinctive) and physiological: if a man with a knife threatens me, emotions of fear are paired to psychological and physiological reactions. In other words, man's cultural environment works upon him as an independent reality. Berger and Luckmann have cogently expressed the general state of affairs of social life: it is the result of a dialectic process of externalization, objectivation and internalization. That is, through language and behavior, man constructs in a process of externalization a symbolic universe, which becomes independent of man in a process of objectivation and controls him because he internalizes this "objective" universe again, making it part of his personality.[8] Institutions are made by man, yet they are independent of him. They are the end product of human praxis and freedom, yet they exert control and determination. Most important of all, institutions provide man with models for action, enabling him to speak, feel, and act in a taken-for-granted pre-reflective way. To a degree, as Arnold Gehlen observed, institutions perform for humans the functions the instincts have in animals.

But the animal is trapped in his instinctive setting, whereas man appears as a world-open (M. Scheler)[9] being, not biologically bound to any specific natural environment. This enables him to create an institutional environment that is adjusted to him and can be altered (or if necessary even neglected) by the human individual. Being born as a biologically helpless, hardly adjusted creature, man turns his disadvantage into an advantage by creating a "second nature" (the socio-cultural reality of institutions), which he can manipulate according to his needs, thus making for an adjustment nature initially had denied him.

Substituting for instincts, institutions thus channel man's behavior, thoughts and emotions. They give his actions and interactions stability, certainty and duration. Most important of all, they provide his emotions with a framework that both *stabilizes* and *stimulates* them. We may therefore assert that human emotions are not only embedded in but also dependent upon social institutions.

Without hypostatizing institutions into "real things," one can, following Durkheim, consider them traditional forms of behavior which transcend the individual and his actions.

Moreover, educational, familial, religious and political institutions make for traditional structures that give human life certainty and stability. They also give rise to functional rationality in interpersonal relationships: because of the institutions, we can expect typical role behavior on the part of others, who expect the same from us. These expectations, having an "objective" ground in the institutional structures, possess the power to coerce our behavior into certain established patterns. This enhances the predictability of our actions. But the expectations also stimulate and inspire behavior! For instance, a believer goes to church not because he believes in an individual and private manner; he believes because he goes to church with others. By the same token, a man does not marry a girl just because he loves her; he also loves her because he is planning to marry her or in fact did marry her. In sum, a definition of a situation becomes real in its consequences (W. I. Thomas) even when these definitions are of an emotional nature. Three examples will help to illustrate this point further.

(1) Romantic love is generally viewed as a most individual erotic emotion. It is, as every sociologist knows, an invention of Western civilization, appearing at the time that the medieval Corpus Christianum began to disintegrate into modern pluralistic society. Its social birth place was among those who lived at the outskirts of medieval society by virtue of their profession, namely the troubadours. As in all pre-industrial societies, marriages in traditional and rural European societies were (until very recently) arranged by the parents in accordance with economic and social deliberations. One married first and usually fell in love afterward.

In the musical *Fiddler on the Roof,* based on the stories of Sholom Aleichem, one of Tevye's daughters decides to marry because she loves a man. This was a revolutionary proposition; marriages in Anatevka had always been arranged by the parents with the help of a matchmaker. After some deliberations, Tevye gives his permission but is subsequently plagued by a most unusual question. He starts to wonder whether his wife actually loves him. When he asks her, she answers in amazement that the question is a silly one since they have been married for twenty-five years and she has given him children and taken care of him for all that time. "If that's not love, what is?" Obviously, in the given situation the question is absurd. But if one insists, it cannot be denied that love is present—not romantic love, but mutual respect and a love that is borne by tradition rather than emotion. If this tradition loses its power, the musical tries to say, everything begins to move. Tradition is like a fiddler on the roof, inviting people to dance. People lose the sound of music and the sense of rhythm if one tears the fiddler off the roof.

(2) Many explanations have been given for the origin of religious rituals. A very suggestive hypothesis was constructed by Arnold Gehlen who interpreted rituals as representations and re-enactments of fearful and extraordinary events.[10] Through the ritualistic (that is, repetitive) re-enactment of the event, anxiety and fear are stabilized in a pattern of behavior that remains under man's control. By performing a ritual dance in which a hunter kills game (obviously a frightening event for Neolithic man), the dancer gets the real event (the hunting itself) under his control. In other words, he gets magical power over the hunting act, and, what is more important, he now has control over emotions of awe, fear and anxiety. Like all patterns of behavior, these rituals acquire a momentum of their own and are passed on to next generations as if they had a reality of their own. By performing the traditional dance, the dancer each time experiences again the emotions of fear and anxiety. The dance summons up in the dancer emotions of religious awe. In a way, all rituals are "storehouses" for emotions that are aroused in man each time they are performed. This is a great cultural accomplishment because the emotions of fear and anxiety, which may overwhelm man outside the cave in nature, have been transported to inside the cave where they can be called for and made fruitful at the times man himself has destined for them in his ritual calendar. Through ritualization, emotions have been neutralized and stripped of their contingency. It seems legitimate to apply this neutralizing and stabilizing function to all institutional patterns of behavior.

(3) Mythology reveals a similar state of affairs. As Mircea Eliade has demonstrated, the myth tells the story of creation: *in illo tempore*, i.e. in primeval, mythological time, the gods

created the universe out of chaos.[11] By reciting these stories
and enacting them in his rituals, primitive man feels himself
a contemporary of the gods and co-creator of the world.
Myths and rituals call up in man religious experiences. The
primitive is a *homo religiosus* only because he recites myths
and performs rituals! In very strong contrast to this stands
our individualized concept of religion.

Eliade always stresses the integrative and stabilizing function of mythology. It neutralizes the arbitrariness of time and
history by transferring them to *illud tempus*.[12] That means,
what happens here and now is not real and essential but a
duplicate of what happened in primeval time, before or during the creation of the world. Myths and rituals transport man
from the here-and-now to this "real" reality of the gods. In
doing so, they arouse emotions of solidarity with gods and
fellow men and emotions of religious fear and awe. It is difficult to determine what exactly caused ritual behavior and
mythology, but, given rituals and myths as traditional "social
facts," one must realize that they possess very strong powers,
which can mold and "create" human emotions of sorts.[13]

If I say that emotions are "created" by transindividual social realities (myths, rituals, or secular institutional behavior
patterns), I mean to say that the biological equipment of
man merely carries the material out of which emotions are
formed by societal institutions. The animal has an innate
biological principle of organization which man lacks. The latter depends on an outside force that imposes coherence on
naturally unco-ordinated feelings, longings, and desires.
Through institutional patterns of behavior, these vague feelings develop into coherent emotions.

It must finally be borne in mind that the institutions and
language of a culture define what fear, pain, sorrow, joy,
hatred and love actually are and which situations call for
which emotions. What is called joy in one culture may be
pain in another, and a situation that calls for sorrow in our
situation may well arouse emotions of fear elsewhere. The
conclusion may be drawn that emotions are not only channeled and stimulated but even defined in their contents by
the traditional institutional patterns of the culture in which
they occur.

We can now draw some conclusions as to the problem of rationality and irrationality in contemporary society.

Human Emotions Vis-à-Vis Abstract Society

Pluralistic society, as we saw in the third chapter, is an abstract society, detached from human experience. The individual in this society has to change the social roles of autonomous sectors continuously, which inhibits an emotional identification with his institutional environment. This society, in addition, requires from him an impersonal bureaucratic attitude, which will, of course, cause an increase in the distance between the individual and modern societal structures.

This severing of the existential bonds between the individual and his societal environment has some important consequences. To begin with, the social institutions continue their own "life" and display an ever-stronger tendency to become goals in themselves. This is an inherent feature of all institutionalization and increases still more in the framework of industrial, capitalistic society. Marx in his theory of reification, Weber and Sombart in their historical analyses of rationalization, made this point the prime object of their interests.

Secondly, modern institutions, detached from human experience, are no longer able to channel and stimulate man's emotionality, throwing the modern individual back on his own subjectivity where the major directives and incentives are lacking. Deprived of the rational control of institutions that traditional man possessed, modern man grows in emotionality, and this emotionality has to be escalated artificially and constantly since the institutional stimuli and controls cannot be replaced by man's biological organism. In addition to this, modern man, becoming ever more aware of bureaucratic rationality and its alienation, is prone to anti-rational philosophies and styles of life, which in continuously alternating fads and fashions are called upon for the satisfaction of emotional and irrational demands. A third consequence must be added to these.

Paradoxically, the separation of man and abstract society

has also led to <u>an increased rationality in man's mental atti-tude toward his institutional environment</u>. As we saw in the third chapter, traditional man lived society, modern man faces it. The former took his social world for granted and experienced it as a traditional and in many respects sacred environment. The latter views his social environment as a neutral force that all too often limits his freedom. It is im-portant to realize, for instance, that the social sciences as a rational interpretation of man and society could not have emerged from a totemic setting. Only if man is relatively detached from his institutions can he reflect upon them and treat them as objects of empirical research. Moreover, a pe-culiar "elective affinity" (Weber) seems to exist between the rationality of the sciences and the rationality of the bureau-cratic structures of modern society. Modernization is not just a function of the rise of empirical sciences, the empirical sciences are themselves a function of the modernization proc-ess of societal structures, which has rendered these structures ever more neutral and rational.

These observations are relevant to an adequate assessment of the rising emotionality in contemporary society. As we saw in Chapter 4, the modern spirit of protest appears to be be-coming increasingly absolutist, displaying all the features of an emotional neo-romanticism. At that point of our discus-sion, I interpreted this neo-romanticism as a reaction to ab-stract society. This is, of course, much too simple. After our analysis of rationality and irrationality in abstract society, we can now draw the conclusion that the irrationality of con-temporary neo-romanticism appears to be a function of the rationality inherent to the social structures of modern society. This means <u>that the romantic revolt against abstract society is, at base, not a genuine revolt but a function of the very alienating structures it attempts to change or to overthrow.</u> If we are serious in our desire to humanize modern society, the spirit of protest seems not to be the way!

NOTES

1. Parts of this chapter have been published as a paper by *Social Research*, Spring 1970 Issue, under the title "Rationality and Irrationality in Pluralistic Society."

2. See, for instance, Max Weber's famous lecture "Wissenschaft als Beruf" in: Max Weber, *Gesammelte Aufsaetze zur Wissenschaftslehre* (Tuebingen: J. C. B. Mohr, 1968), pp. 582–613.

3. See for a discussion of the relation between constructed models of science and common sense in the "natural world," Alfred Schutz, "Common Sense and Scientific Interpretation of Human Action," *Collected Papers*, Vol. I, pp. 3–48.

4. As to these methodological reflections, Weber's theory on rational understanding of irrational behavior remains still unsurpassed. Cf. his "Knies und das Irrationalitaetsproblem," *o.c.*, pp. 42–146.

5. For the present discussion, the distinction between non-rational and irrational is not very useful. Karl Mannheim, however, introduced the valuable distinction between *functional* rationality (–irrationality) and *substantial* rationality (–irrationality). Substantial rationality is man's capacity to see in an intelligent act of thought interrelations between facts and events in a given situation. (Cf. Pareto's residue of combinations.) Consequently, behavior is substantially irrational if it does not stem from such an act of thought but is generated by drives, impulses, wishes and feelings. Functional rationality, however, is the organization of a series of actions in view of previously defined goals. Viewed from the standpoint of the observer, Mannheim adds, functional rationality displays a consequent calculability. Cf. Karl Mannheim, *Man and Society in an Age of Reconstruction*, p. 53. It is clear that the definition given by me restricts rationality to the functional kind. There is no need, according to me, to call this functional rationality "technique" as Jacques Ellul seems to profess in *The Technological Society*, transl. by J. Wilkinson (New York: Vintage Books, 1964).

6. Arnold Gehlen has remarked that even the modern arts have become "political": abstract art or serial music are identified with politically "left" positions. Arnold Gehlen, *Macht einmal anders gesehen* (Zuerich: Fontana Verlag, 1954), p. 16.

7. I am indebted throughout this book, but particularly in this chapter, to the philosophical anthropology of Arnold Gehlen. By the concept "anthropological nature of institutions" is meant the notion that the human condition is predominantly determined by cultural institutions. Cf. Arnold Gehlen, *Urmensch und Spaetkultur* (Bonn: Athenaeum Verlag, 1956).

8. Cf. Peter L. Berger and Thomas Luckmann, *The Social Construction of Reality*.

9. Max Scheler, *Die Stellung des Menschen im Kosmos* (*Man's Place in Nature*).

10. Arnold Gehlen, "Ueber die erstehbarkeit der Magie," in *Studien zur Anthropologie und Soziologie*, pp. 79–93. Cf. also his *Urmensch und Spaetkultur* (note 7).

11. Mircea Eliade, *Aspects du Mythe* (Paris: Gallimard, 1963).

12. Mircea Eliade, *Cosmos and History*.

13. Music performs a similar function and has therefore always been a crucial element in ritual performance. A last survival of this "mythological" function of music is to be found in film music. Hearing the music of a certain motion picture (say, the Lara theme from *Dr. Zhivago*) the emotions of the original drama are evoked again and come "alive." Romantics are, of course, particularly aware of this. Background music in the plays of Anton Chekhov, for example, is a means to evoke the melancholy of the past and the sadness of unfulfilled desires. It is in the same frame of reference that one could interpret rock music and other emotional forms of musical expression popular today among the younger generations. Incidentally, only a time like ours, in which the rationality of institutions oppose the emotionality of individuals, can produce such contraries like electronic music (technologically rational) and beat music (emotionally irrational).

7

THE NEED
FOR INTELLECTUAL ASCETICISM

Introduction

In the preceding chapters I have attempted to interpret some of the main signs of our time by showing how the process of modernization has led to an abstract society in which the individual has lost the existential ties that bind him to his social structures. There are, of course, conflicts in pre-modern society, but they are mostly of a petty nature and can easily be resolved. If dissenting groups gain a real momentum and conflict grows into a structural reality, as it did in the movements of the Cathars in the twelfth century and the Reformation in the sixteenth century, we may conclude that the cultural configuration within which these conflicts occur is in a process of transition or even of decay. But apart from such rapids in cultural history, pre-industrial man receives his identity and freedom from an encompassing meaningful reality, integrated by the bonds of religion and tradition.

Modern man's life lies between relatively autonomous and institutionally isolated sectors. In addition, the bureaucratic attitude is required of him: he must be rational and efficient if he is going to keep up with the pace of modern society. His socio-cultural environment, being abstract, is not able to provide him with meaning, reality and freedom. The definitions of his world are not in harmony. Said W. I. Thomas: *"There are rival definitions of the situation, and none of them is binding."*[1]

The sixties witnessed a strong protest against abstract society, particularly on the part of those who have to live in it for the remainder of this and the beginnings of the next century. For various reasons, adolescents are more susceptible to the spirit of protest than adults are. Most important of all is the fact that the modern adolescent goes through a period of transition from childhood to adulthood that is often stretched out over a time span of more than ten years. Although the modern adolescent is physically ripe in his early puberty, he must be *culturally adult* before he can accept a responsible position in society. For those who go through high school, college and often also graduate school,[2] such a position is not available until approximately ten years after completion of physical adulthood. Recently adolescents have refused to wait until society grants them cultural adulthood. Still in a situation of dependence (often called "tutelage"), many of them *appropriate* their adulthood through opposition.

Furthermore these adolescents are often confronted by society with demands that do not concur with their status of dependency. For example, they have to serve in the nation's army and, in the case of the United States, many of them are called upon to fight in a cruel war. They are also allowed to vote for political leaders. Thus, they fully share in the decisions made by an adult world but are called "kids" if they assume an adult responsibility and say "no" to these decisions. To give a concrete example: the war in Vietnam is planned by adults but executed by adolescents. As long as they are in college, these adolescents are "kids," but they are "men" when they serve in Vietnam. In other words, adolescence is a non-defined period between childhood and adulthood. Society stresses one or the other aspect at its own convenience.

Understandably, the adolescent protests against this situation. He accuses "the system" and its "power elite," but whatever he is protesting against, it remains unresponsive. Viewed in this perspective, it is no wonder that he either takes the road inward or engages in violence. On the road inward, he needs ever-stronger stimuli and shocks, since he rejects all institutional enticements. On his road toward violence, he must escalate his actions, since he lacks clear alternatives to justify his deeds. The violent rebel hates "the system," wants its destruction, but has no alternatives for the present—mainly because nobody knows what precisely "the system" is, to begin with! He must thus convince himself by his very actions. We discussed these various escalation processes within the modern spirit of protest and called them collectively "romantic absolutism."

Constructing three types of protest, Gnosticism, Anarchism, and Activism, we found that the primacy of *homo internus* is common to all three. Man's authenticity is believed to remain after his social roles have been stripped off. There is admittedly a great difference between the Gnosticist searching for meaning and reality within his own psyche and consciousness and the politically involved Activist who dreams of a new society without alienation. But both share a fundamental distrust of, if not hatred for the institutions of modern society. They no longer seek incentives and directives from societal structures: the Gnosticist takes the road inward in an artificially activated escalation of his emotionality, whereas the perhaps more sophisticated Activist searches for the intellectual shocks of an "existential (relevant) knowledge" and beyond that for mere action.

The preceding discussion was largely diagnostic. In the present chapter, I will venture to suggest remedies. It is another sign of our time that our diagnoses are usually stronger and more convincing than our proposed remedies. We all know by and large what is wrong, but we hardly know what to do about it. Most social scientists intentionally avoid proposing alternatives to the critically analyzed situation. What is worse, they consider such proposals unscientific moralism and beneath their dignity. I shall not conform to this trend but will frankly state my thoughts on these matters. Meanwhile, I fully realize the weaknesses of the position I shall assume.

As might be expected, I will once more take up the homo duplex theorem, but this time in a socio-ethical, normative frame of reference, drawing conclusions from the preceding discussion. I used the homo duplex theorem as theoretical background for my observations and interpretations. I now return to it for some concluding remarks. By this procedure, I admittedly get out as "result" what I initially put in as "theoretical model." The homo duplex theorem has been the guiding thread throughout this book. Therefore, the following "conclusions" merely repeat the initial presuppositions and do not have the value of empirically derived conclusions.

Social philosophy as a speculative discipline is necessarily redundant. It gets out of its discussion what it initially put into it. The empirically minded sociologist may reject social philosophy for this very reason. I, for my part, do not share his scientific fundamentalism. To me, social philosophy is useful as addition to empirical sociology, as long as it does not conceal its redundant nature. One has put the rabbit in the hat and there is no sense in fooling oneself and the audience by hiding this simple fact. However, something happens to the rabbit while it is in the hat. Social philosophy tries to make its initial presuppositions more plausible by logically interrelated speculations based upon empirical observations. Or in terms of the present study, I posed the homo duplex theorem as philosophico-anthropological principle. I then tested it by applying it to the situation of man in contemporary society, attempting to demonstrate that abstract society has polarized homo duplex in one direction, while man himself has polarized it in another. The former wants the socially conformed *homo externus;* the latter reduces himself to *homo internus.* It was implicit throughout this discussion that I would call for a reconstruction of homo duplex in modern society. But I do so only after some very fundamental considerations, which were often founded upon empirical material. The "conclusions" are therefore the *further reflected upon* and *more crystallized* expression of the initial presupposition, namely that man's nature is embedded in social ambiguity.

Incidentally, redundancy might well be a fundamental aspect of all scientific enterprises. We cannot, of course, discuss here the nature and function of scientific hypotheses, but I mention just one element: hypotheses are generally constructed before scientific research begins. After several manipulations, these hypotheses are declared to be "true" until further empirical evidence proves the opposite. This means that science can never attain Truth. It can only arrive at evidence. This evidence is declared to be truth-until-further-notice. Although there are distinct differences, social philosophy does not deviate very much from this procedure in the sciences.

Seen against this background, social philosophy might not

be as worthless as many empirically minded sociologists may think. But there is no way of proving the point. In the final analysis, it is up to the reader to decide whether the analyses and interpretations in the foregoing and the "conclusions" in this final chapter make sense and are useful for a better understanding of the peculiar position of modern man in an abstract society.

Man's social ambiguity polarizes, and not abstract society, but the individual suffers from this. It stands to reason then that all attempts to *humanize modern society* should focus upon this polarization. In one way or the other, man has to maintain his double nature, if he is going to survive as a human being. We cannot, of course, turn the clock back. All reactionary Gemeinschaft utopias and "back-to-nature" dreams are doomed to fail because they blindly deliver the individual to the coercive forces of abstract society. We have to learn to maintain our social ambiguity within the parameters of contemporary society. Meanwhile, abstract society, autonomous as it may seem, is not our Fate. The sorcerer's apprentice created an environment which gained momentum, began its own life, and perhaps got out of hand. Nevertheless, the apprentice should not lose his head. He should remember that *he* brought this environment to life and that he can *control* it if he knows how. At the end of this chapter, we will raise the awkward question of whether the apprentice is at all able to control his world without the help of a sorcerer who has the knowledge necessary for such control. At this point, I merely stress the simple fact that it is the apprentice who has created this world of "living things."

The fundamental problem for modern man, it seems to me, is how he may *regain control* over his life and his environment. This, today, is his greatest challenge. Such practical problems as birth control, pollution control, preservation of nature, etc. clearly indicate man's ongoing attempt to keep the "second nature" with which he has surrounded himself under his control.

There are four main problems:

How to control social coercion

How to control intellectual segmentation

How to control human emotionality

How to control man's social ambiguity

After everything that has been said, the reader will understand that this emphasis on restraint and control is not related to the wish to repress freedom and creativity. On the contrary, I view man's regaining of control over himself and his environment as one of the fundamental prerequisites for genuine freedom and creativity.

How to Control Social Coercion

Rather than Mannheim's question, "Who plans the planner?" we should ask ourselves today, "How do we control social control?" Rather than running amok, we should attempt to regain control over social coercion. Rather than withdrawing from it into private subjectivism, we should try to beat "the system." This is difficult because the forces of social control in contemporary society bear some very peculiar features. William Faunce has formulated it as follows:

> The impersonality of the(se) constraints in industrial societies contributes in an important way to the sense of powerlessness. If the only source of oppressive control is a totalitarian leader, he can be overthrown. If the source is an entire way of life, revolution is a less effective response. The idea that "you can't beat the system" expresses the impotence of people confronted by a rationalized and impersonal system of social control.[3]

This rationalized and impersonal nature of social control is illustrated by the simple fact that one cannot *complain* successfully in modern society. Society is so complex that the complainant cannot find the appropriate person to whom he can address his dissatisfactions. The unhappy lot of the *consumer* is a perfect example.

In traditional societies, the transaction of buying and selling was based upon personal service and good quality of products and was a matter of face-to-face interaction. If service and quality failed to satisfy the customer, he could direct his complaints to the responsible person. The shopkeeper might fail to recognize the fairness of the complaints but the buyer at least knew how and to whom to address them. Contrast this with the self-service in a streamlined supermarket. The buyer who has complaints about the quality of products is gently sluiced through different layers of responsibility and authority. If he decides to follow the road to its bitter end, he may find himself in the office of a manager who appears to be so detached from the pedestrian act of buying and selling that the original complaint suddenly seems irrelevant and even silly. By then, it is easy for the manager to move the customer, reimbursed or not, from his office to the street without losing for one moment the uncommitted smile imprinted on the faces of higher bureaucrats for the sake of Public Relations.

During the transition from traditional to modern society, the *service model* has undergone a radical transformation: unless he belongs to the very rich, the customer is not king any more, but part of a bureaucratic wheelwork in which efficiency and functionality are economically more profitable than the personal satisfaction of individual demands.[4] In this situation, supply is no longer determined by demands, demands are increasingly conditioned by supply. The consumer is controlled in a very pervasive way, but, like all control in abstract society, the control is "invisible." It is the work of the famous "hidden persuaders." How is the consumer going to regain control over his consumption?

During the sixties, a very interesting thing happened. Officially organized consumer control, stimulated and protected by the government, proved to be largely inefficient—probably because government and business are too closely knit together these days. Only a crusade organized by a single individual gave consumers back a certain power over the market. Where government-appointed institutions failed, Ralph Nader demonstrated that the individual in abstract society can regain effective control—and in a strictly legal manner! Nader has achieved some very fundamental protections for the modern consumer. He does not lament about alienation, he plays "the system" and has beaten it on some very important points. Indeed, he was one of the most hopeful signs of the past decade, a rare example of an *individual* in modern society who has not been overpowered by its abstract structures.[5]

Like the consumer, the functionary in a large bureaucratic organization or the blue-collar worker in a huge factory is trapped in a strict hierarchy and unable to express his dissatisfactions about work and working conditions. Being in a precarious position "somewhere" on the hierarchic scale, white- and blue-collar workers do not have much opportunity to vent their complaints or to fight for elementary justice. If they were to decide to express themselves, they would meet considerable problems in finding their way through the "organized irresponsibility" that seems to characterize all large-scale organizations today. They would, moreover, risk their very positions in the hierarchy, since they would be showing other interests than the rather narrow duties required by the system. The individual is controlled in a very concrete way, but the forces that control him remain "invisible" or are at least buried in the web of a bureaucratic labyrinth where they are unsusceptible to influence from individuals.

Blue- and white-collar workers alike are thus subjected to new forms of injustice. The novelty lies in the fact that it is the *individual* rather than a collectivity (like the "working class") who suffers. Traditional labor unions are not equipped to fight this injustice. They themselves have become large-scale bureaucratic organizations dominated by the principles of rationality, functionality and efficiency. They simply cannot afford the luxury of humanitarianism toward individuals. They too have to be "realistic."

Here again a more individual approach seems necessary. This has partially been realized by the Scandinavian invention of the *ombudsman* who functions as neutral mediator between individual functionaries and the system.[6] The ombudsman is not part of the hierarchy and has to listen to the complaints of individual functionaries on different levels of the organization. The ideal ombudsman is an objective listener and "outsider" who relays individual dissatisfactions to the appropriate offices where he also defends their cause. This is, from the sociological point of view, a fascinating phenomenon. The ombudsman is installed in the bureaucratic organization as a kind of non-bureaucratic individual who wanders through the structures as a "stranger" defending the justice of individual workers. Whether he will successfully find his way through the labyrinth and defend the justice of certain claims and complaints remains to be seen. If the role of ombudsman is not played by a charismatic and inventive individual, he will easily end up as counselor or social worker, listening to complainants and functioning as a safety valve put on the system by those in power. In any case, we see here once more the attempt to regain control over institutional constraints through an individual rather than structural (or organizational) approach.

Emotional revolt against the coercive forces of abstract society is inadequate mainly because the romanticist, as we have seen, becomes the victim of rationalized manipulation almost as easily as the conformist. Bureaucracy's pervasive control cannot be fought by emotions. But "structural" solutions, like labor unions defending the rights of the workers, have by and large also become ineffective—particularly in regard to the elementary rights of the individual. The unions were doomed to bureaucratize. Indeed, the AFL-CIO is a perfect example. It is not opposed to the Establishment but a rather powerful part of it.[7]

At his point, I would like to recall the fundamental question raised by Theodor Geiger in opposition to existentialist lamentations about alienation: *Are the structures of modern society wrong, or is modern man still unable to live in them?* Must we focus primarily on a reconstruction of modern institutions, or should we work on man's capacity to live in this society and to encounter consciously its abstract structures?

A one-sided answer to this question is, I am aware, not without grave dangers. If one focuses on the structures of society only and claims that the present malaise of democracy results from structural diseases, one easily ends up in what I propose to call "structural fetishism"—the inability of man to see institutions for what they really are, namely mere means for the realization of human life. Structural fetishism views institutions as goals which are either to be defended at all costs or to be destroyed no matter what human price such a destruction entails. Structural fetishism occurs from the far "right" to the far "left." Needless to say, its very nature conditions it to trample upon the most elementary rights of the individual. It supports the autonomy of the institutions in pluralistic society and simultaneously impairs the modern individual's ability to cope mentally and emotionally with the totally new phenomenon of abstract society. Modern man has to learn to master the forces of control *on the level of consciousness first,* before he proposes structural changes. One-sided "structuralism," it seems to me, fails even to recognize this possibility.

On the other hand, a one-sided emphasis upon the need for individual reconstruction may easily result in unrealistic moralism. Poverty is a structural disease, charity an inadequate cure. I do not hesitate to acknowledge that modern society needs structural changes, particularly on the economic and political levels, and especially in view of its relations to the so-called Third World. Several drastic measures are necessary to prevent a range of catastrophic conflicts, in comparison to which the problems we have been discussing appear to be luxuries of a relatively safe society. But I am also convinced that such structural changes can proceed successfully only if modern man's consciousness is sufficiently equipped to meet the problems that an abstract society imposes on him. It seems to me that we today do not meet the terms for this strenuous and responsible encounter, despite all our lamentations about alienation.

Man today, more than ever before in history, has to learn consciously how to live in his society, how to master mentally and emotionally the forces of control he has created. This requires a *new form of consciousness.* There are two important prerequisites for such a consciousness. First, modern man must learn to regain control over the process of segmentation that has affected his life and his mind in the form of specialization and professionalization. Secondly, he must learn to control his emotionality and find a balance between rationality and irrationality. These issues are dealt with in the next two sections.

How to Control Intellectual Segmentation

Not only the structures of society, but also man's consciousness has become segmented in the process of modernization. We discussed this in the third chapter and called it "intellectual Taylorism." Modern knowledge, scientific as well as common-sense knowledge, has been fragmented into various sectors of discourse with very little communication between them. This is evident in the sciences (specialization) as well as in the sphere of labor and work in general (professionalization). Specialists and professionals are experts in only a small portion of possible knowledge. Outside their limited field of expertise, they are naïve, helpless, if not plain uneducated. Moreover, as we saw in the third chapter, there is enough evidence to suspect that most specialties and professions have exhausted their various fields of expertise and the main work left to be done is compiling abstractions: debates on methodology, theories about theories, piecemeal revisions of existing theories, and research for the sake of research (or because an attractive grant was available). In the different branches of culture (sciences, arts, music, literature, sport, etc.), specialization and professionalization have brought human consciousness to a level of abstraction never before reached by man. The scientist has become slave of his methods, the performing musician has sacrificed musicality for ever-greater technique, the sportsman has exchanged the playful spirit of the game for a grim struggle against the chronometer, and painters and sculptors alike compete nowadays for ever-newer techniques. As a result, they have all delivered their particular field of expertise to the meaninglessness of ever-expanding abstractions.

Again, structural measures can keep this process of intellectual segmentation within certain limits. But it is on the level of individual consciousness that the real change should occur. I would like to emphasize, for example, the wholesome role *the amateur* could play. In our era of professionalization we have forgotten that much creativeness and quite a number of innovations have come not from professionals but from amateurs. For instance, in sociology, Max Weber was and still is one of the greatest sources of innovation, but he was never a professional sociologist in the strict sense of the word. He was a typical representative of a breed of intellectuals who might be called "professional amateurs." He was not only economist and sociologist, but also jurist, historian, political scientist, historian of religion, and philosopher. He knew a great deal about music and literature, and was fluent in several languages. Obviously, he was not a specialist in any of these fields.

Goethe, another remarkable professional amateur, allegedly said that dilettantes greatly promoted the causes of science and technology because they knew how to combine *play* with *seriousness*.[8] The dilettante, as the etymology of the word indicates, has pleasure in developing certain ideas and in solving certain problems. He is committed to his cause, not because he searches for fame, prestige and professional acknowledgment, but because he has pleasure in pursuing it. The rat race of competition, the grim fight for the improvement of existing records, the stress on methods and techniques and perhaps most important of all, the hunger for money—all these characteristics of the modern professional are alien to the true dilettante. He plays the piano because he loves music, he paints because he takes pleasure in the composition of figures and combination of colors, he does scientific research because he is inquisitive, he engages in sport because he likes to measure his own physical endurance against that of others.

Understandably in an age of professionalization, but nevertheless regrettably, "amateurism" and "dilettantism" have become pejorative categories, used condescendingly by those who are determined to defend their own small field of expertise. Meanwhile, if we really have exhausted our specialties, the spirit of the amateur may bring some very wholesome changes. Among other things, professional amateurism might produce a truly interdisciplinary approach in the human sciences because it would not be restricted by professional blindness but would tend to combine various specialties. This is not an endorsement of mediocrity. On the contrary, much of our professionalism has resulted in mediocrity, whereas the true amateur might open new vistas, new approaches, fresh impulses and perhaps even new substance. He transcends the narrow parameters of a specialty but is not a system builder. He resembles those famous Renaissance men who knew nothing very specific but quite a lot in general.

All attempts to change formal education in contemporary society, it seems to me, should focus primarily upon this aspect. University reform is a perfect example. The discussions on this topic center almost exclusively around changes in organizational structures and in curriculum patterns. This is an outgrowth of our fetishistic belief that all the pains of modern society can be alleviated by changing structures and organizations. But such structural changes, necessary as they are, can be successful only if a change in man's consciousness takes place simultaneously. All structural reforms of the university must be paired to reform of consciousness if they are to be at all efficient. This reform of consciousness can be achieved through education and is relatively independent of all structural and organizational circumstances. That means that we can begin on it immediately, irrespective of all the structural changes that have to occur. The reform of consciousness I am referring to consists primarily of deprofessionalization and aims at the promotion of professional amateurism. The prerequisite for this is a radical abstinence from competitiveness and longings for professional prestige. This, again, is only possible in the fundamental attitude I shall call "intellectual asceticism," which leads us to the next issue.

How to Control Human Emotionality

In a thorough and ongoing educational attempt (that is, by secondary schools, colleges, universities, mass media and various forms of adult education) modern man has to learn how to cope with the problems of an abstract society. Not emotional romanticism and its directionless involvements, but a new attitude and a new consciousness are required if man is to survive in a human way. What I envisage here is a new rationality (as attitude and form of consciousness) that is able to understand rationally and relativize consciously the very constitution and functions of modern society—a sort of "sociological imagination" which refuses to take either social institutions or human emotionality and irrationality for granted. I call this new rationality "intellectual asceticism."

Its foremost feature is that it refuses to reduce human life to the level of emotionality. Economic and political interests maintained by power groups are in themselves irrelevant to the intellectual asceticist, although he will support actions against these interests if they endanger the meaning and freedom of the individual. However, he is aware of the human need for institutional frameworks. He therefore strives for structural reality, intersubjective meaning and socially sustained freedom. This means that he will support change and revolution if these three fundamental co-ordinates of human life can be improved institutionally, but he rejects protests for the sake of protest and rebellion for the sake of romantic utopias and anti-institutional dreams.

Intellectual asceticism opposes emotional absolutism by stressing the need for institutional structures, but it does not promote conformism to or compromise with existing institutional orders. On the contrary, it strongly advocates a certain rational detachment that views institutions as what they really are, namely human creations dependent on the will and the actions of human beings. Indeed, intellectual asceticism is a kind of *sociological stoicism* in that it refuses to endow society with metaphysical features. Societal institutions are, after all, merely means for the channeling and enticing of individual existences. This is a simple statement, but it has to be made in a time in which institutions are viewed as either the holy shrines of democracy or the sources of alienation.

Since it is firmly rooted in rationality, intellectual asceticism is rather far remote from all mystic forms of asceticism. It is more related to lucid sociological consciousness than to the intentional irrationalities of Christian mysticism or Indian philosophy. It is, most important of all, anti-gnostic in that it knows that man's interiority has its point of gravity outside itself, namely in other men and in the structures of society.

At this point, we recall W. I. Thomas' Creative Man as a

personality type that develops not as a static result but as a process between the "producing factor" and the "produced result." Creative Man is neither a Philistine who conforms to the given circumstances, nor a Bohemian who revolts aimlessly against them, but a homo duplex who, often by trial and error, tries to realize his existence within the framework of social institutions. He will act against institutions if they threaten to reduce him to an obedient functionary with Philistine attitudes, but he rejects simultaneously the attitude of the Bohemian who dreams of an existence without any institutional coercion. Under certain circumstances, he might join the Bohemian protest, but he will reject all absolutist demands and extremist utopias. The Bohemian, of course, will call him a Philistine, just as the Philistine will often consider him a Bohemian. But he is neither.

In the final analysis, the Bohemian and the Philistine are both emotionally tied to the structures of society: to the Bohemian, institutions are targets to be attacked or even annihilated, to the Philistine, they represent his highest values to be defended by all means. As we saw in previous chapters, abstract society has increasingly polarized in these two directions. It is important to realize that Creative Man sees institutions as mere means for the realization of human existence—unavoidable means, that is. His intellectual asceticism keeps him from any form of absolutism that turns goals into means and means into goals. Whereas the Bohemian and the Philistine are equally bound to the structures of society, Creative Man manages to maintain his independence.

Intellectual asceticism as a form of consciousness that keeps man's emotionality in balance with rationality, must not be confused with the rather old-fashioned rationalism Geiger proposed as the solution to modern irrational romanticism. At the end of his *Demokratie ohne Dogma* (1952), which was mentioned in the first chapter, Geiger calls for a continuation of the process of rationalistic Enlightenment, which, according to him, has been interrupted by a long period of romanticism. He distinguishes between an intensive and an extensive Enlightenment, the former being the rationalism of the sciences, the latter the rationalism of the people in general. In his opinion, intensive Enlightenment has continued to de-

velop within the relative seclusion of the sciences, whereas
extensive Enlightenment has been interrupted by romanti-
cisms of several kinds. Through a general diffusion of
rationalism, Geiger hopes for a continuation of extensive Enlightenment today. He obviously got caught, however, in an
outdated form of positivism which dreams of the power of
Science and of Progress by means of human rationality. As
a result, he seems unable to see the romantic roots of all rationalism, despite its initial anti-romantic intentions. The idea
of Progress, for example, as a process stimulated and regu-
lated by human rationality, has led to various irrationalities
(e.g. "Natural Law"). Moreover, the rationalist belief in
progress can have fatal consequences. Albert Salomon proved
this point in *The Tyranny of Progress* (1955) when he said:
"The logic and tyranny of progress gave to the world the
progress of total tyranny."[9] Despite his claims of the opposite,
the combination of rationalism and positivist value-nihilism
(*"Wertnihilismus"*), proposed by Geiger as the solution for
the pains of our time, seems to be full of the very dangers
he wants to fight.

It is certainly not old-fashioned rationalism that can restore
in modern man the fundamental dialectics of the homo duplex, but rather the sociological stoicism that refuses to reduce man to an emotional *homo internus* and simultaneously
maintains its critical stance vis-à-vis the controlling demands
of abstract society and its attempt to reduce man to a mere
homo externus. Peter L. Berger has called this kind of intellectual detachment "ecstasy," i.e. the ability to step outside
the "taken-for-granted routines of society." "Ecstasy," he observes, "transforms one's awareness of society in such a way
that *givenness* becomes *possibility.* While this begins as a
state of consciousness, it should be evident that sooner or
later there are bound to be significant consequences in terms
of action."[10]

Ecstasy is an important ingredient of intellectual asceticism, making for a detachment that leaves room for more
adequate praxis. As *intellectual* asceticism, this form of consciousness is neither irrational nor emotional. But as a form
of *asceticism,* it is not rational in the positivist sense of the
word. The real homo duplex will escape the traditional op-

position of rationality and irrationality. His consciousness, remote from each form of onesidedness, will pair a new rationalism to a new asceticism. It is a rational mysticism which the Austrian poet and novelist Robert Musil has called "the other condition."[11]

How to Control Man's Social Ambiguity

We must, finally, come to grips with a last group of problems. Since it transcends the limits of our present discussion, I can only mention it. A full discussion would require another book. I must warn the reader, however, that what follows lies beyond the scope of the social sciences and social philosophy. I mention it with necessary hesitancy.

One could argue that, at bottom, man has to learn how to control his very social ambiguity itself. The legitimate question then arises whether he will be able to do so *on his own account*. Modern man is a promethean creature who has acquired a well-nigh almighty power over nature and mankind. But is this "Prometheus unbound" at all able to maintain the delicate balance of his interiority and exteriority without external control? This is a crucial question, because if the answer is negative one might conclude that he is equally unable to maintain the balance of his power.

One step further, one could argue that modern man has been doomed to "deify" his psyche and consciousness as the realm of authenticity, and to "satanize" the institutions of society as the realm of alienation, *after he murdered his God*. After the "death of God," solemnly announced by Nietzsche, the Sacred as the realm of absolute meaning, utter reality and absolute freedom had to be erected within man's immanent world. As we have seen, within this immanent world he reduced the absolute once more to his own interiority. The human self, no longer relativized by a transcendent God, becomes an idol—a "thing" to be elevated and worshiped.

In the Old Testament, Jahwe alone and his deeds in history are absolute and sacred. Everything else—men, nature, and societal institutions—is profane and relative. According to this faith, sex is not absolute. It, therefore, could not accept any erotic cults or temple prostitution. The Old Testament is not "against sex" but it rejects the absolutizing of sex. Neither were social institutions, like the family or the monarchy, viewed as absolute. It, therefore, never developed an ancestor cult or instituted a divine kingship. Israel's theocracy was founded, not primarily and originally upon a powerful priesthood, but upon a prophetic faith in a transcendent God who is immanent only in his historical deeds. Neither nature nor society—those relatively petrified realities confronting the individual—is absolute, according to the faith of ancient Israel, but history is because it presents the stage on which God's actions with man occur.

In this respect, Israel was unique among the religions of the world. Everywhere else, "religion" has always served as *the* deifying mechanism absolutizing almost every aspect of human life. As its history demonstrates, Israel has always had a hard time not returning to visible idols and relying solely on an invisible God. As a matter of fact, it was often seduced into forsaking this transcendent God and returning to the religious certainty of idols and immanent gods. It then automatically began to absolutize human existence, nature and societal institutions. In other words, it then became just another religion.

The God of the Old Testament became the God of Christianity and underwent many essential changes. Nevertheless, throughout the history of the Western world, the one essential feature of Jahwe has always been retained: *God was the exterior point of gravity for man.* Through his God, Western man was enabled to keep his social ambiguity in balance— that is, until he murdered his God.

Nietzsche tells us the story of the madman who announces the death of God to an amused audience. Man has murdered his God, but he seems not to realize what the consequences of his deed are. The madman cries out that man lost his stability and sanity after he killed his God. We have disconnected the earth from the sun, he says. And now we fall, fall eternally, into all directions, backward, sideward and forward. There is no above and below any more. We roam around as through an everlasting nothingness. Empty space is gazing at us.[12]

The death of God has deprived modern man of a stable reference point outside himself. In his search for the absolute, he now knows no limits. He surrenders to his own *hybris*, like those tragic heroes in the plays of Sophocles, Aeschylus, and Euripides. Modern man idolizes his own history (Progress), his own being (Humanity), his own psyche (Authenticity), and condemns any restrictions on these "absolutes" as alienation. Thrown back upon himself, man is eventually destined to the tragic split of gnostic dualism, in which he opposes a self-imposed authenticity to alienation.

Thus, the death of God has led to the birth of many idols, man himself being the most prominent one. Rather than liberating man from religion, the event has delivered him to a never-ending search for absolute meaning, utter reality and absolute freedom within the immanent world—a gnostic search that will not find its fulfillment. The experience of alienation will gradually be heightened, as in a spiral movement.

In this situation, it seems to me, man has the choice of either forsaking the search for the absolute and settling for the relative, or continuing the search. These are, respectively, the stoic and the religious options for modern man. If he decides to continue his search for the absolute, as seems to be the case in contemporary society, he again faces a double option. He can either try to find the absolute within the immanent world, deifying human realities in a kind of religious humanism, or he can adhere to the Judaeo-Christian faith in a transcendent, absolute God who saves him from enslavement to self-produced idols. Despite the fashionable opinions about the death of God, we could consider the possibility that ancient Israel's God is alive. After all, his death could be as much a human projection as his existence generally was! It would require a prophetic movement to bring this very awkward idea to the attention of modern man. Such a movement is certainly not to be expected from "progressive" and "modern" theologians who prefer to swing with the tempers of our time.[13]

But we might have to face the terrifying fact that man stands alone in the universe. In that case, the burden of social ambiguity rests upon his shoulders. He will need all the sources of wisdom not to surrender to his emotionality and its gnostic search for the absolute but to settle for relativity in a firm and stoic attitude. Such an intellectual asceticism requires a temperament under control and a very strong character.

It is not fashionable in the contemporary social sciences to deal with problems of social philosophy and social ethics— let alone of theology. But then, ours is a time of fads and fashions. If intellectuals are worth anything today, they should at least liberate themselves from everything fashionable. What counts are the issues not the fads. The issues we have presently dealt with call for a combined effort on the part of sociologists, social psychologists, historians, social philosophers and theologians. Scientists, philosophers, and theologians have been in conflict long enough—even to the extent of mutual negation. But modern man has now entered a stage of history in which provincial attitudes can no longer be afforded, certainly not on the part of those who call themselves intellectuals.

The present study is an attempt to transcend the customary intellectual divisions in order to contribute to a cultural analysis of modern man's position in an increasingly abstract society.

Montreal,
December 1969

NOTES

1. W. I. Thomas, *The Unadjusted Girl,* 1923 (New York: Harper Torchbooks, 1967), p. 82.
2. The relation between student unrest at graduate schools and the increase in the enrollment in graduate studies has not been sufficiently studied yet. There are several factors involved here. I mention two of them. First, a contributing factor to student unrest is a gradual devaluation of university degrees, having a particular effect on the highest level (master's degree, and Ph.D.) with the highest amount of pressure. The college B.A. has become what a high school degree was before, the M.A. resembles ever more the original B.A. and the Ph.D. is on its way to become the equivalent of the traditional M.A., which in turn calls for post-graduate studies. This cannot but lead to tensions and dissatisfactions. Another factor in the U.S. is the

draft. Allegedly, many students enroll in graduate studies in order to evade the draft legally. They are more refugees than future scholars and naturally prone to activism.

3. William A. Faunce, *Problems of an Industrial Society* (New York: McGraw-Hill, 1968), p. 103.

4. See M. Horkheimer, "Feudalherr, Kunde, Fachmann: Das Ende des Maerchens vom Kunde als Koenig," in *Die Zeit* 19–47, November 20, 1964. A good discussion of the historical change of service is A. L. Mok's "Is de service op zijn retour?" in H. A. Becker, ed., *Dienstverlening en Publiek* (Utrecht: Erven Bijleveld, 1966), pp. 53–65.

5. Cf. *Time*, December 12, 1969, pp. 67–76: "The U.S.'s Toughest Customer." For Nader's successful drive against the automobile industry, see his *Unsafe at Any Speed* (New York: Grossmann, 1965).

6. Cf. Faunce on the ombudsman in a similar discussion: *o.c.*, p. 104.

7. Werner Sombart mentions this fact already in 1906 in his remarkable study *Warum gibt es in den Vereinigten Staaten keinen Sozialismus?* 1906 (Darmstadt: Wissenschaftliche Buchgesellschaft, 1969).

8. Richard Friedenthal, *Goethe, Sein Leben und seine Zeit* (Vienna: Buechergilde Gutenberg, 1965), p. 343.

9. Albert Salomon, *The Tyranny of Progress*, p. 104.

10. Peter L. Berger, *Invitation to Sociology*, pp. 136 f. Cf. also his *Precarious Vision* (New York: Doubleday, 1961).

11. Translation of "der andere Zustand." Robert Musil, *Der Deutsche Mensch als Symptom* (Hamburg: Rowohlt Verlag, 1967), p. 52. See also his novel *Der Mann ohne Eigenschaften* (Hamburg: Rowohlt Verlag, 1952).

12. Friedrich Nietzsche, *Die froehliche Wissenschaft*, § 125 in *Gesammelte Werke*, Band II, pp. 126–28 (Muenchen: Carl Hanser Verlag, 1955).

13. See in this context Peter L. Berger, *A Rumor of Angels: Modern Society and the Rediscovery of the Supernatural* (New York: Doubleday Anchor, 1969).

INDEX